46 YEARS AFTER...
"THE SIGN"

A JOURNEY...

...your ears will listen to these words behind you, "This is the Way, walk in it." (Isaiah 30:21)

LANNI FIDES

46 Years After ... "The Sign"
Copyright © 2022 by Lanni Fides

All Scripture verses and some reflections are from The New Community Bible, Catholic Edition, St Pauls Publications @2008 and are used by permission - Society of St Paul, Strathfield, NSW Australia.

The accounts in this book are based on actual events. Some names have been changed to protect privacy.

All rights reserved. No part of this publication may be reproduced, distributed, or transmitted in any form or by any means, including photocopying, recording, or other electronic or mechanical methods, without the prior written permission of the author, except in the case of brief quotations embodied in critical reviews and certain other non-commercial uses permitted by copyright law.

tellwell

Tellwell Talent
www.tellwell.ca

ISBN
978-0-2288-7907-7 (Hardcover)
978-0-2288-7908-4 (Paperback)
978-0-2288-7906-0 (eBook)

Table of Contents

Dedication vii
Acknowledgements ix
Introduction xi

Chapter 1: Wedding Bells 1
   1. Nuptial Blessings and Dramas 1
   2. Prejudice and Judgement 8
   3. Honeymoon: Postponed 10
   4. Stephen's Promise 12

Chapter 2: Education and Professions 14
   1. Highlights of High School Days 14
   2. College Days: Love is in the Air 18
   3. My Beloved Professions: Teacher and Librarian 22

Chapter 3: God's Plan and Divine Providence 27
   1. Vocation and "The Sign" 27
   2. God's Gift of Life 41
   3. Stephen's Greener Pasture 45
   4. Homecoming: The Prize of a Family Being
      Together 48

Chapter 4: Our Family Is Getting Bigger 53
   1. Three Angels from Heaven 53
   2. We Have to Go 57
   3. Stephen's New Business Venture 59

Chapter 5:   The Value of Spirituality in One's Life 63
   1. A Family that Prays Together, Stays Together 63
   2. Our Spiritual Life as a Couple 67
   3. My Personal Spirituality 69

Chapter 6:   God Works in Mysterious Ways 72
   1. Migration Opportunity 72
   2. Dilemma: My Father's Illness 76
   3. Medical Check-up Mix up 78
   4. Goodbye Tatay 83

Chapter 7:   Farewell to our Beloved Motherland 88
   1. Tatay's First Death Anniversary 88
   2. Flights vs Financial Woes 91
   3. Nuptials of Liam and Evelyn 92
   4. Departure Blessings 94

Chapter 8:   New Land of Hope and Mission 98
   1. A Migrant Family's Divine Blessings 98
   2. Stephen's Health Scare 103
   3. Our Priceless Castle 109
   4. Unified Family as a Working Team 112
   5. Family Mission 116

Chapter 9:   Fruits of Faith, Love and Sacrifice 120
   1. Love Until It Hurts 120
   2. Growing Pains: Trials and Triumph 125
   3. Peace and Contentment in the Family 129
   4. Holidays in the Hospital 131
   5. Giving Back God's Generosity 135

Chapter 10: Death in the Family..137
    1. My Family Ancestry's Short Lifespan 137
    2. Who Can Comprehend God's will?...................... 141
    3. How Do I View Death?..144

Chapter 11: Travels and "Holydays" with God 148
    1. Bucket Lists Before Retirement............................148
        a.   Holy Land Pilgrimage Tours – 2011 150
        b.   Marian and Miracle Sites of
            Faith Pilgrimage Tours – 2014.................... 153
        c.   Steps of Saint Paul – 2016........................... 159
        d.   Graces of Eastern Europe – 2019 167
    2. Travel Missions Accomplished through God's
       Providence 172

Chapter 12: The Glory of Retirement 177
    1. God said, "It's Time to Retire."..............................177
    2. Have Goals Set Before Your Retirement 180
    3. Pandemic: Blessings and Challenges.....................184
    4. The Honour and Splendour of Retirement 187

Conclusion 193
About the Author 197

Dedication

to

my loving husband, Stephen
our beloved children and families:

Jasmine & husband Jeremiah, children Jean & Jermaine
Matthew & wife Raelyn, children Raphael & Mae
Lily & husband Marty, children Christopher & Maya

my loving sister Jade
All relatives and friends

and

You my readers

Acknowledgements

*Deepest gratitude for the motivation,
inspiration and support of:*

my loving family

*Catholic Church Parish of St. John 23rd
Stanhope Gardens
and its Ministries of the Word and
Special Religious Education,
NSW, Australia*

*Couples for Christ Australia
and its Ministries
my Chapter-Seniors' Household,
NSW, Australia*

Society of St. Paul, NSW, Australia

Introduction

... I closed my eyes and fervently prayed to God for a "SIGN" ... I deeply contemplated God's plan for me...?

I have written this book to proclaim to the whole world God's unconditional love and divine providence to His people. To prove this truth, I have revealed my beautiful life's journey in 46 years after God gave me "The Sign" to follow His plan for me. This testimonial book shows God's power in the midst of life's challenges and trials. God always works in mysterious ways and has full of surprises for us beyond our expectations!

It is my aim to assure readers that, in my experience, God never abandons us.

Thus says the Lord, "Have no fear, for I am with you; be not dismayed, for I am your God. I will give you strength, and bring you help, and I will uphold you with my right hand of justice." (Isaiah 41:10)

God is faithful and never leaves us.

It is sad to see around us, that some people do not believe this, due to the busyness of the world and focus on wealth, fame and power. God is totally irrelevant in some lives! This book absolutely proves this wrong in my life and testimonials! "God is all we need in our lives" is the message I wish to convey through my words and experiences, with the hope that it would affirm to God's followers and somehow touch a non-believer!

"Hold on God's power, trust in Him and follow His plan" is my inspiration in sharing my life's experiences particularly in choosing my state of life which is generally, the largest segment in a person's life time. My revelations manifest the importance of always focusing our eyes, heart and mind onto God's will and plan for us.

"The Sign" is a symbol of my total and complete surrender to God, which unfolds my life's memoirs as a whole, mainly on marriage and family life. It is an absolute trust on how I let God be the controller in my journey. I just let go and let God!

That's why this book came into conception in order to showcase God's love, guidance and providence in my blissful marriage after the Holy Spirit divinely prompted and guided me to "THE SIGN" in approval of this remarkable man to be my beloved spouse.

This year 2022 marks our 46 years of delightful marriage!

Are you keen to know what was the sign all about? What happened in all those 46 years?

Well, it is time to sit back, relax and read over a cup of tea or coffee. Enjoy!

It is my sincere hope that readers in all states of life, find my life's journey, in some ways, helpful and inspiring in order to get by in their everyday challenges and realise God's unconditional love and faithfulness to His people.

Are you ready for this journey?

Lanni Fides
16 May 2022

Chapter 1

Wedding Bells

Whether you turn to the right or to the left, your ears will listen to words behind you, "This is the Way, walk in it."

(Isaiah 30:21)

1. Nuptial Blessings and Dramas

April 2, 1976

It was nine o'clock on a beautiful Sunday morning, the sky, a bright blue, peppered with gentle, wispy clouds, sporadically spread. A white bridal car stopped in front of our Spanish style two-storey house. The driver stepped out, hurriedly going up to see my father, whom I referred to as "Tatay" (which is the Tagalog word for "Father"), calling out, "It's time to go or else we will be late."

Finally, Aunt Torie finished fixing my simple white bridal veil, making sure it spread all over my white silk gown. Tatay entered my room and loudly repeated what the driver said.

So, we had to go and I slowly walked down the stairs towards the bridal car, as I prayed and hoped that we will arrive on time for the wedding mass. "Help us Lord, I don't want to be late," were the words I repeated on the way to the car for I didn't like dramatic entrances where all eyes focused on me!

It is very common in a small village, where everyone knew everybody, that naturally, everyone knew of events, especially special occasions. As I expected, there were many spectators on the street waiting for the bride to enter the bridal car, ready to judge the bridal gown, shoes, hair style, make up, etc. This is where all opinions and judgements are ripe, if all passes to their taste or standard. I just ignored all whispers and mumbles of words, when I couldn't help but overhear a man, who spoke loudly and clearly to the man next to him saying, "I cannot fathom why she chose that man she is marrying today. I am sure, there are others better than him!" The other man answered, "Maybe, she was forced into this marriage." Another woman who heard their conversation added, "What security will she get out of this marriage? If I were her mother, I would not approve of this marriage!"

So painful to hear all these prejudices and judgement! I prayed for patience and peace, as I was already so worried because we were running late and these people's negative commentaries added to my anxiety. With God's grace, I kept my peace, managed to calm my nerves, as I held tightly onto my rosary. My inner self totally ignored the negativity, instead, I held my head up high, clinging to the promises of God and His approval to this man, who will soon be my husband.

It was a one-hour drive to reach our destination, the wedding set to begin at 10:45 am. I loved the serenity in the car, as I was seated by myself at the back and Tatay was at the front, engrossed in conversation with the driver. This gave me time to collect my thoughts and reflect on all the events leading up to this memorable day, which will soon affect the totality of me, my whole being, soon to be a married woman.

I clearly remembered those words from Mother Superior, "My child, God wants you to save your father and two brothers from the darkness of sin. This is your mission for now and you are always welcome to come back in the future." I went home that day like a lost child after the depressing rejection on my application to be a nun. I felt my whole body go numb and lifeless. All I felt was a total desperation and desolation and just wanted to disappear for a while to breathe freely. I stayed in my room, went to bed in tears and then fell into deep sleep. Miraculously, I woke up a new revitalised and re-energised person, as I prayed my morning offerings. I felt that my guardian angel bestowed her magic wand on me, so I could be somewhat protected from the "sorrow" and instead be enveloped in "joy."

Despite my unsuccessful application to be a nun, I remained as a high school teacher and elementary school librarian in the same school run by the Benedictine Sisters and enjoyed my profession.

After a year since that time, so many shocking incidents happened which had changed my life dramatically. My two brothers, Kuya Nico and Liam were still at the height of their vices, addicted to alcohol and drugs. ('Kuya' means older brother in Tagalog).

One time, I was in a Parents and Teachers Conference, when a policeman asked for me and I was in shock when he told me about Liam's arrest and was locked up in jail! Kuya Nico on the other hand, was totally engrossed with his group, regularly had drinking sessions and completely ignored his studies. When Tatay learned all of these terrible incidents, he wasn't strong enough to face the challenges, so, he refused to go home as per his usual routine on weekends, instead he chose to stay in the city with his friends to drink, be happy and forget the troubles at home! He completely abandoned us!

This was my breaking point and I needed someone to lean on! I did, however felt the presence of God and Mother Mary embracing me, which in turn, gave me peace and a feeling of serenity.

That weekend I was just so lonely in our empty house, when my former college classmate and my fellow college teacher, Stephen dropped by and I felt at that very moment the importance of his presence, especially at this time of family turmoil. During our college days, on a regular basis, Stephen visited me on Saturdays, asking for assistance with his various researches and projects, which he failed to do because of his work as janitor and driver of the college's director. He worked hard on these two jobs, in exchange of his free education from high school to college. We became close friends, and I looked up to him like a big brother, admiring his self- determination to educate himself through persistence and perseverance. Being one of fifteen children, it was a struggle for his parents to send them all to school. So, he applied to be a self-supporting student to work different jobs as what the school needed in return for free education. He successfully passed his application and assigned him these two jobs! His personality was a total contrast to my two brothers' character, and his hard-working attitude absolutely gained my full admiration and respect towards him. So, as I opened the door and saw Stephen, my heart leapt with joy and in that instant, did not feel so alone any longer in that empty house, void of my brothers and father!

The sound of the church bells suddenly shook me out of the trance of recollecting the events and looking down at my watch, with great relief, it showed 10:20 am. Praise God, we made it in time!

Fr. Ambo, the parish priest came out to check if everyone was present to witness this holy ceremony uniting a couple to be one in the sacrament of Matrimony. I quickly glanced at the bridal entourage and I instantly noticed Stephen's restlessness. Everyone was present, except his parents! At exactly 10:45am, the priest signalled the pianist to start playing the bridal processional music, even without Stephen's parents. I absolutely felt Stephen's frustration and disappointment - his parents' failure to witness this most memorable part of his life – his crowning moment!

As the priest gave the blessing, ended the ceremony of the holy sacrament of marriage, and started the crowning moment! God crowns the bride and the groom as His prince and princess and eventually they become the priest and priestess of their own family and clan in the future! That was how I envisioned this moment in our lives, an epitome of God's crowning of this marriage!

Holy and solemn was the ceremony, especially with that background music of "AVE MARIA" during the portion of 'exchanging of vows' and 'kiss the bride.' There were sounds of sniffles, as few guests shed tears, as you do at a wedding, the guests likely reminded of their own wedding days, or some dreaming of their own wedding day in the future. The end of the ceremony ended with loud applause as a sign of overwhelming joy and happiness for two people united by God and transformed into one in love, peace and mission!

"The three persons in a marriage is the formula in a successful marriage," were the words of Fr. Ambo which I still remember to this day, during our pre-nuptial seminar.

The third person being God must always be in the centre of a marriage, and this "formula" got implanted in our hearts throughout the last 46 years after "the sign" and till the end of time.

After the mass, Fr. Ambo, the parish priest, who was Tatay's first cousin, invited us to the little hall, just behind the church for morning tea. He knew that we left our respective houses so early and all must be exhausted and hungry, as reception lunch at the nearby restaurant won't be served till 1:30pm. Stephen and I were speechless with this unexpected act of kindness and generosity from our uncle-priest, so I hugged him and completely taken by surprise again, when he handed me an envelope with money inside and words written 'as a support for your new life for Christ!" To add more flavour of goodness to my story, he gave us free services with the use of the church and said, "You will be both servants of God and faithfully repay Him in that way!"

When everyone was refreshed both physically and emotionally, we started to get ready to leave for the wedding luncheon. All of a sudden, we heard noise along the hall's corridor and finally, Stephen's parents arrived with some relatives and apologised for their late arrival! I squeezed Stephen's hands tightly, for I could see that although he was happy his parents were here, he could hardly contain his disappointment of them missing the actual ceremony, signalling him to be calm and just accept the apology and move on. With the grace of God, he did! Drama averted. Thank you, Lord!

2. Prejudice and Judgement

Sometimes people can be cruel; talking about and judging other people become a second nature. One inspirational speaker once said, "Miserable people love to talk about people's miseries and faults in order to feel good about themselves."

Yes, people would often misjudge Stephen, seeing him as a son of a poor farmer who was unable to send his children to school due to deprivation. He was a self-supporting student, who worked double jobs as a janitor and driver in order to gain free education, and a man with no material wealth to offer for security for the future. These were the main attacks made by the people from our village who knew my family, well known as the 'orphans' because of the early death of our mother, who left behind three children: Liam, a one-year-old baby, me, the middle child being only seven years old, and Kuya Nico, eight years old.

I simply brushed away all the negative judgement and opinions of people. Sadly, some of these judgemental people were my own relatives who looked at the value of material wealth more than good personality and character. The more that these negative ratings were pointed towards Stephen, the more positive points were added to his profile in my heart. The number one person, and the person who mattered most to me at the time, who was opposed to Stephen and who judged him harshly was Tatay! He never liked Stephen and whenever he was under the influence of alcohol, he would call Stephen a boastful man, and not good for me at all! I ignored all those comments and kept telling Tatay that I did not intend to marry anyone.

I assured him that Stephen was just a classmate and a friend, who was like an older brother to me. Tatay thought that he was "wooing" me because of his regular visits on Saturdays, sometimes bringing with him produce from his home farm when he was lucky enough to go home amidst the pressures of his studies and multiple jobs. In truth, Stephen had never mentioned anything about love and Tatay didn't believe me at all!

I had a helper boy named Rene, a seven-year-old boy, whom I sent to school, and sponsored his schooling until he finished high school. He just lived across the road from us and sometimes stayed at our house to help me with my chores as well as running errands for me.

One Saturday night, Tatay was again in one of his drunken states, and I asked Rene to get a message out to Stephen not to visit me, because of Tatay's condition. I was worried that he might say bad things and act nastily towards Stephen. So, Rene went and relayed my message as per my request.

But of course, Stephen insisted on seeing me, ready to bravely face Tatay. As you can imagine, my father wasn't happy at all, totally ignoring Stephen, as if he wasn't there. He drank some more, playing his loud music even louder, blaring from his beloved "QuadraSonic" stereo.

To make things worse, when Tatay got tired without a single word, he plopped himself down on a sleeping mat right in the middle of the "salas" or lounge room, where we were sitting, simply laid down and started snoring loudly. Stephen and I looked at each other and just found it hilarious, for we both knew and understood what Tatay was doing.

Tatay started to feel insecure towards Stephen for he started to realise the sincerity of this man, perhaps the reason why he started acting so indifferent lately. Wait a minute, I said to myself. Why would Tatay be jealous of Stephen, when he didn't even say the word 'love' to me at all! That's bizarre, don't you think? In my naivety, I intended to clarify this to Stephen in his next visit.

3. Honeymoon: Postponed

At the wedding luncheon, I'd noticed everyone was satisfied with the delicious food served and happy with the excellent service of the waiters, until someone started to make unmistakable sounds of glasses being tinkled, a signal for the groom to kiss the bride which Stephen did, lovingly and gently! The toastmaster called for the toasts to begin and raised his own wine glass to start the well wishes! Everyone was happy on the dance floor and singing along with the band. What a simple, but beautiful and meaningful celebration of love and new life!

It was nearly six o'clock in the afternoon when we arrived home. This time Stephen was with us in the bridal car, along with Tatay and Jade, my ten-year-old step sister, who had been living with us for the last four years, and loved Stephen so much, like she loved her real older brother.

Liam, my sixteen-year-old younger brother and Kuya Nico and his wife Norma were already at home waiting for us. Everyone was still full because of the late lunch and I didn't think we were able to have dinner that night.

We all changed out of our wedding attire to something more comfortable while Tatay gently played soft music and put the kettle on. He asked Stephen and myself to sit at the porch with our cups of tea. Oh, this gesture coming from Tatay was rather unusual, so I could not help but feel a little nervous! I knew that he wanted to talk to Stephen about something important. To my surprise, Liam and Jade joined us at the porch. Jade started crying because she wanted badly to come with us to our Baguio trip the following day and Liam did as well!

My goodness, this was to be our honeymoon, I told myself in disbelief! I had noticed Tatay holding his head in pain, so, I gently touched him and felt that he was slightly warmer than normal. Noticing my concern, he said, "I am alright, it's nothing, just enjoy tomorrow." I'd sensed his sincerity with his wishes, but at the same time, worried about leaving him. Then all of a sudden Stephen seriously spoke up and said, "It must be the heat and exhaustion.

Tatay, please have some rest, while I go and buy medicine." He hastily went to the pharmacy and luckily, it was still open. The next day, the honeymoon trip to Baguio was called off.

4. Stephen's Promise

Stephen woke up early morning to fetch the village doctor and they arrived at midday. The old doctor, who had been our doctor since I was a little girl, opened his professional bag and pulled out the blood pressure cuff to measure Tatay's blood pressure and check on his body temperature. I saw the doctor's unhappy reaction and asked what he found. His blood pressure was high along with his body temperature. So, he handed Tatay the prescriptions for medication in order to stabilise his condition. We kept an eye on Tatay the whole day. Surprisingly at night, he stood up and walked towards the window and sat on a chair. He called me and requested Stephen to see him. I felt that he had something important to tell his son in law.

These were the words of Tatay as related to me by Stephen. "You know that your wife is my pillar and mainly in charge of this household with Jade, Liam and Nico and his wife, Norma. If you plan to leave us, I will be losing my pillar and this household will collapse." Wow! I was extremely amazed hearing what Tatay thought of me. I could see Stephen contemplating on Tatay's words. "I humbly request that you and your wife stay here at this ancestral home, for I can't envisage that this house will remain intact without my daughter." Stephen sincerely accepted his father in law's request and promised him to keep his word. Tatay was so delighted to hear his son in law's promise and I had noticed, from that moment, the sudden change of his actions towards Stephen. It seemed that he started to accept him as his real son and became comfortable to ask him favours, such as fixing some carpentry work at home, along with other odd maintenance work. One time, they were both together in a hardware shop, buying some timber and paint and started to do some small renovations at home. You see, Stephen is rather the handy man and he knows almost every bit of electrical, mechanical, painting, plumbing and carpentry theories, which made my old man happy and content.

The old ancestral home became more alive, as everyone got occupied with their own roles and responsibilities. I couldn't imagine the house would ever be filled with life, it was completely opposite to what it was used to; now bright and noisy instead of having been previously dark and silent. We had Tatay only on weekends, because he worked from Monday to Friday in the city and during the whole week, Stephen and I, my younger brother Liam, and young sister Jade, Kuya Nico and wife Norma permanently stayed here.

So, the household consisted of the original three, now had doubled up into six during the week and seven on weekends!

CHAPTER 2

Education and Professions

*"Trust in the Lord with all your heart;
do not rely on your own insight. Let
His presence pervade all your ways, and
He will make your paths smooth."*
(Proverbs 3:5-6)

1. Highlights of High School Days

1966-1970

Do you agree that generally high school years are the most exciting and adventurous years in a person's lifetime? I would absolutely agree! But on the other hand, this is also an alarming period where one could end up with the wrong crowd and set aside one's focus on goals and aspirations.

Adolescence is the phase of life between childhood and adulthood, from 10 – 19 years old; the age of teenagers, generally with 'happy go lucky' and 'come what may' attitudes. I recalled Aunt Nina's words when I was eleven, "When the time comes, and you have reached your teenage years; you stay with good boys and girls and choose your peer group and sets of friends. Birds of the same feather flock together." I didn't quite understand what she meant at that time, but faithfully adhered to her words of wisdom through the years.

Elisa was my classmate from year one until high school and became my best friend right up to this present time. She was a mathematician and so no wonder she ended up as an accountant after college graduation and later on, pursued her career as a lawyer. During our high school years, she always gave me a helping hand when I needed extra help in mathematics, as I wasn't good at this subject. Thank goodness, I excelled in all my other subjects which certainly contributed to the required score for my partial college scholarship.

Elisa also lost her father at a young age, similar to when I lost my mother when I was almost seven years old. We shared the same trauma towards the loss of a parent, that's why we had developed a very close relationship like that of real sisters.

In high school, we formed a group of seven, which consisted of five girls and two boys like brothers and sisters, helping each other accomplishing our projects and individual assignments. Our little group all lived geographically close to each other, which made it quite convenient to meet up at each other's houses in order to finish our projects. We would often go together to the fields and catch frogs and insects to preserve them for our science projects. It was a great adventure to explore the dry creeks and rivers to collect big flat stones and rocks to build a pyramid for our history projects.

This is also the period where teenagers start to have crushes and where "puppy love" begins, which to me, during that time, only meant admiration towards someone's good character and excellent performance on a certain subject. I knew that because I also admired one of my classmates who was a math wizard. He had a talent which I didn't have, and I was so fascinated by his amazing ability in solving algebraic equations! Others ended up frustrated because they misconceived admiration as falling in love and later on, lost their focus on their studies.

To be in the top model section (which is what was referred to as a high performing class) of fourth year high school wasn't easy, especially if you aimed to be among the top ten of the model class. There was a tight competition to be in this class because of the super talents and high level of intelligence of the class members. Rigid tests and qualifications were strictly required in order to be in the 'model section.' I had above average grades in all subjects, all except mathematics. So, I thought of a strategic way to compensate my weakness through the other subjects which I extremely loved and enjoyed. I excelled in Home Economics and Music. Our Home Economics teacher gave us a project to crochet curtains for windows, walls and doors or covers for dining tables. The score will be based on the length of the finished crocheted items. I strategically chose to crochet hanging curtains for both windows and doors. Every afternoon after school until night time, I sat down crocheting while listening to music. The faster the music was, the quicker my fingers moved!

During the submission of our projects, I had to ask Kuya Nico's help to carry the bundles of finished crocheted items for me. My teacher was in total shock when I presented her my completed project of forty metres of sixteen hanging curtains fitted for four windows and four doors! She could not believe what she saw and asked me, "Are you sure you did all of these, with no help from your mother or anyone?" I stood up that little bit higher and with confidence, answered her, "Yes Madam, all by myself! I lost my mother when I was almost seven years old and I am very sure, she is proud of me in heaven!" The teacher hugged me and sincerely apologised. I ended up earning the highest score on record!

I loved Music! That's why I decided to choose it as an alternative subject in place of Physical Education. I felt like I was in heaven each time I strummed the 'bandurria' a stringed musical instrument given to me as my designated instrument in the school band.

We participated in competitions against other school bands in the region and never came home empty handed, coming home with awards and trophies! Some neighbouring schools and organisations in the province occasionally invited us to entertain their special events which always ended up with the audience providing feedback of great satisfaction and enjoyment. Our patient and understanding Music teacher, Mr. Franco, played an important role in leading and supporting me to end up in the top ten in my class. You may ask why and how? I was in total disbelief when he gladly voiced out, "Because of your diligence, punctuality, passion and excellent performance as a soloist, I am rewarding you a deserving 99% mark for your final grading!" So, these two subjects absolutely pulled me up to the top of the ladder and I proudly graduated high school with the distinction of being among the 'Top Ten Graduates' of our batch!

Praise God Almighty!

2. College Days: Love is in the Air

1970-1974

"*P*arting is such a sweet sorrow" is a famous quotation of William Shakespeare which is very appropriate for goodbyes and separations; a mixture of emotions of joy and sorrow. I felt this when some of my closest friends went to the city universities, while some of us stayed in the same college.

One of my closest friends in high school was Leni, who used to go home with me during lunch break. We enjoyed each other's company, as we talked about life and our plans for future. She kept telling me how poor they were and cried unconsolably at one stage to the point where I could not pacify her. Then she calmed down saying how lucky I was, even without a mother compared to her own life of misery. I became curious and asked her a lot of questions, until she opened up about all her pains and sorrows.

Leni was a self-supporting student, one of fifteen children whose parents were not capable of sending them to high school. Fortunately, this well-known college, owned by philanthropists, offered free education which helped disadvantaged families in exchange of work and services for the school. Now that we had graduated high school, Leni was accepted in one of the universities in the city as a self-supporting student again. She was over the moon, when she shared the good news to me. Sadly, she left without saying goodbye. After one week, surprisingly, I received a long letter from her. I felt this enormous happiness for what she'd achieved, while I read her inspiring stories and adventures in the city.

Meanwhile, Elisa and I stayed in the province and pursued our dream courses in the same college. She wanted to be an accountant, so she enrolled in the course of Bachelor of Science in Commerce. My dream to become a teacher led me to the course of Bachelor of Science in Education. Our busyness in our respective fields of studies did not obstruct our constant communication and catch up on weekends. The year had quickly passed and we were both satisfied with our academic performances.

Everyone was happy to see each other after a semestral break and eager to start another year. I was seventeen and the youngest in my class, because I went to school earlier than any one of them. In second-year college, mainly the basic subjects were included in the curriculum of all courses like English 1-4, Theology, Economics and others, which means there was a mixture of students in different fields of studies and years.

On the first day, my first class was English 2 consisting of around 16 students representing different courses and years. I chose to sit at the back of the room, due to my farsightedness, when a dark, haggard-looking man in his early twenties, wearing a neat light blue polo shirt, entered the room, walked towards the back and saw the empty seat beside me, politely asked, "May I sit beside you?" "Yes of course," was my quick answer.

The professor explained the syllabus of our subject, objectives and expectations from us. He started some intensive reviews from the previous English subject and I found him more efficient than my last professor, as the class was completely silent, attentively listening to his lecture. After half an hour, he made an announcement that the College Director needed to see a student by the name of Stephen in his office. The man seated beside me stood up and left the room.

So, now I knew this man's name. Intuitively I felt that there was something mysterious about him.

The bell rang signalling the end of the first class and I proceeded to the next. I couldn't wait for the lunch break so

I could see my best friend Elisa where we can exchange quick updates with how we were both going on our first day, as sophomores in college. We sat under the shade of an acacia tree having lunch of sandwiches, bananas and cold coconut juice to fill up our empty stomach and quench our thirst, especially with this midday 35 degrees Celsius heat. To my surprise, Elisa called out to that man Stephen, when she saw him hurriedly passing by, "Kuya Steve, wait, here is your sandwich and drink."

Elisa was also a self-supporting student in the college working as a bookkeeper. I gathered from her that my classmate in English 2, Stephen, was accepted as a self-supporting student too with double roles as a cleaner and at the same time, driver of the college director. The way Elisa quickly narrated his background, had answered almost all questions in my mind.

At twenty-three years of age, he was only a freshman in college because he stopped studying after his elementary school and helped his father look after the farm for almost six years. Wait for the biggest surprise! Elisa happily informed me that Leni, our former high school classmate and Kuya Steve are siblings and among the fifteen children! I was dumbfounded and felt this indescribable feeling in my heart! (Kuya is also a polite address to an elder brotherly like person). What a small world, indeed!

Two years quickly had passed, Elisa and I were already in our last semester and ready for graduation. We both excelled in our classes, getting the highest scores in our examinations.

In the meantime, Kuya Steve became a regular visitor at each of our houses asking help to catch up with his projects and researches which I just happily passed on my old researches with some amendments. He was so thankful for both Elisa and myself for all our assistance.

We understood his difficult situation especially when the college director needed his service, even in the middle of examinations. I felt so sorry for this hardworking man, but I knew one day he will reap bountiful rewards from all these sacrifices and surely will find glory! God never sleeps and knows everyone's heart desire!

Both Elisa and I graduated with the highest honours representing our own degrees and moved on to the next stage of applying for a job. Praise God for all His goodness!

3. My Beloved Professions: Teacher and Librarian

April 1974

Two months before my graduation, I mailed application letters to the nearby private Catholic Schools applying both as a teacher and librarian. I prayed for God's guidance and blessings regarding my applications. In my daily conversations with Him, a fleeing thought quickly entered my mind with the notion that whichever school responded first to my applications, will be my choice, in the event that I was to get more than just the one reply. I felt in my heart that God approved that approach, because I felt happy, content and peaceful after my prayers.

Indeed, God is good! After two weeks, I received several positive responses and noted the dates of receipt being faithful to what I said in my prayers. I was so delighted to receive a reply from Saint Mary's Academy, a private Catholic School run by the Order of Saint Benedict Nuns, in which teaching was their charism. The Academy's principal responded to my application two days ahead of the rest, with a date for an interview, so I immediately replied my availability to attend the proposed date and time for the interview.

I believed that God did indeed guide me all the way through the ordeal because everything ran smoothly and accordingly.

I felt this overwhelming feeling of happiness, my eyes filled with tears of joy upon finally receiving the letter of acceptance from the Principal of Saint Mary's Academy. I was to be a high school teacher for half the day and an elementary school librarian the other half of each day. I was over the moon with that kind of arrangement! To my surprise too, the principal requested that I start library projects straight away, right after my graduation!

Thank You, Oh Lord God!

At home, I knew that Tatay was highly proud of my achievements, taking pride in the honour of standing beside me on stage with the Dean of Education, as he vested upon me the highest medal of honour in my degree.

Words were not enough to express my gratitude for everything that had transpired through God's guidance and providence, especially my instant reward of immediate employment.

Praise be to God Almighty!

Meanwhile, my two brothers stopped studying and got into trouble with alcohol and drugs.

Tatay wasn't happy at all. His frustrations with his two boys, pushed him more to drink with his group of drunken friends, just to forget his disappointments. Tatay had a very weak character of never facing the music, rather, evading the truth to forget the pain and worry with alcohol, his best friend.

I was at Saint Mary's Academy working at the library, when all of the sudden, a year two boy in his boy scout uniform, approached me and gave me a little package, saying that an old man instructed him to give it to the elementary school librarian. I was puzzled and asked the boy where the old man was and he replied that they were gone. I noticed that he said 'they' and not 'he', meaning there were more than one person, so, I asked him again what the old man looked like. He said, "Very old with white hair and glasses seated at the back seat of the car." That was more than enough information for me to conclude that, that was the director of the college with Kuya Steve!

"What's going on?" I wondered to myself.

That weekend, Kuya Steve visited again and I took my chance to ask him questions about the little package, consisting of lunch, which they dropped the other day at the school.

He said that it was the Director's idea to buy me lunch and I just simply accepted that. Kuya Steve noticed my quietness and sadness. It was his turn to ask questions. As soon as he uttered the words, "Are you okay?" I couldn't control myself and I burst into tears. With tears flowing freely, I felt a cleansing and unloading of the heaviness of my heart's burden, heavy with my family's mess.

His regular visits at home gave him the chance to know all the dramas in my family. I looked up to him as my older brother, and had me opening up to him for brotherly advice. I knew that he befriended Liam, to guide and push him in the right direction and for that I would be forever thankful to him!

One time, Liam told me that Kuya Steve gave him some driving lessons, which to me was a smart move to win his attention and affection in turn. He knew that Liam, a sixteen-year-old adventurous boy, would be very interested to learn how to drive. So, on some weekends they spent time together, driving around, Liam happily helping Kuya Steve with his odd jobs.

They developed a very close friendship, in which I later noticed Liam was even closer to him than our older brother Kuya Nico. I felt so peaceful knowing that Liam spent a lot of time with Kuya Steve for I knew he will give him the right advice and guidance in life. But it seemed that the bad influence of Liam's peer group was stronger and he was still being pulled towards the wrong path. I surrendered Liam and Kuya Nico's wrong-doings to God's power to open their eyes and one day be enlightened to walk through the right path.

Chapter 3

God's Plan and Divine Providence

"Make known to me Your ways, O Lord; teach me Your paths. Guide me in Your truth and teach me, for You are my God, my Saviour; I hope in You all the day long." (Psalm 25: 4-5)

"...I am with you always, until the ends of this earth." (Matthew 28:20)

1. Vocation and "The Sign"

December 8, 1975

As my own personal life ran smoothly according to God's plan, my two brothers were fast drowning in the opposite direction, consumed with a lifestyle fuelled with drugs and alcohol. Tatay's drunkenness and womanising ways, which resulted in multiple affairs, aggravated the chaos in my family. I found that I could not stand the presence of each of them, to the point where I didn't want to go home anymore. I found refuge at the Benedictine Convent and would often stay there until they were about to close the gates.

It was a total contrast of atmosphere being at the convent, where there was peace and serenity as opposed to being at home seeing my father and brothers in the throes of sin, getting deeper in the pit of darkness. In despair, I even thought of leaving them, like abandoning a sinking ship!

With great sadness, I asked Kuya Steve not to visit anymore on weekends, for I needed time to find myself and discover the right road to take from that period in my life. Since I was a young girl, having the utmost respect and love for the nuns, I would often imagine myself as one. I told him the truth, that I had requested an audience with the Mother Superior and right away, she agreed to meet me that coming Friday. Stephen knew from the start of our friendship, of the religious vocation I contemplated following as soon as I settled my family's mess. I saw his face go red and he simply said, "Rest assured that I will pray for you and your intentions. I just want you to be happy. May God bless you."

That Friday, the Mother Superior rejected my application to become a nun.

Two months quickly passed and my library looked impressive with newly built book shelves aligned against two walls facing each other, filled with newly bought books which just arrived the previous day. I placed some colourful posters outside the door to attract the children to enter the spacious, shiny wooden-floored room. In the middle of the room, I laid down a very big, inviting and colourful round rug, with bean bags, designed for younger children to sit on comfortably while reading. I placed a 'Please remove shoes' sign. This was good for those children who were on long breaks and had the time to let themselves be lost in a book. In all corners of the room, there were also several small, colourful chairs to choose from, suited for children on short breaks and who were not comfortable to removing their shoes.

I received an overwhelming approval and appreciation from the principal and teachers!

The Teachers-Parents Association were invited to the opening and blessing of the new elementary library. They were impressed and gave it a five-star rating, pledging to shoulder the total expense of purchasing children's encyclopedias, globes and some more dictionaries! That was a memorable and joyful day of reaping the hard-earned labour of love!

At nearly five o'clock pm, I was ready to go home after a long day, to rest my tired body, but restful soul, when the Mother Superior cheerfully entered the room and gave me a great big hug to show her appreciation of the successful event. She said, "I am so proud of you, for not losing your focus, despite your non-acceptance to enter the convent. My daughter, as I have said, with open and loving arms, you are most welcome to apply again after five years."

We parted joyfully, I went down the stairs and entered the side door of the church to visit and pay homage to the Blessed Sacrament. After my reflections and prayers, I heard a sound of a bird chirping, trying to get out of the church. As I stood up, I heard its chirping sound beside me as if following me towards the door. I let it followed me and as soon as I opened the door, swiftly it flew up to the sky with its cheery cheerful chirps, as if saying,

"Thank you for my freedom!"

Again, that night after my prayers, I thought of all that had transpired during the day.

Everything came together successfully and I felt accomplished! I felt joy and peace as well, after my conversation with Mother Superior, as a feeling of total acceptance of the rejection to a religious vocation; for a noble reason of saving my family from drowning.

My eyes were opened to the truth. That I was helpless, fearful, weak, and acted like a coward faced with my responsibility. I then realised and felt that God had a different calling for me, to a different state of the life I thought I wanted. God sent that bird to convey His message of freedom from doubts saying, "Have no fear, for I am with you; be not dismayed, for I am your God. I will give you strength, and bring you help. I will uphold you with my right hand of justice." Isaiah 41:10.

Then I fell into deep sleep as I heard the chirping of birds and the rippling, bubbling sound of the streams in the woods.

On the third Saturday of December, I attended the vigil mass at six o'clock in the afternoon so, I could have the luxury of a sleep-in the following morning. I invited Liam to accompany me to church which he surprisingly nodded his agreement to. I was so delighted to be with him and prayed fervently to God ... that was the start of his turn-around!

Since the time he was released from jail, due to some drug issues, he kept me updated with his daily activities. He told me of his continuous driving lessons with Kuya Steve, whom I haven't seen in what seemed like ages! Knowing that he spent a lot of time with Kuya Steve, honestly brought peace and joy to my heart!

After the mass, Liam rushed to go because he had a meeting with Kuya Steve, which was set at seven o'clock for more driving lessons, in order to be ready for his Monday's driving test. So, I let him go, and I made my way home to have our family dinner with Tatay and Kuya Nico, without Liam. I remembered him saying that he will have dinner, with Kuya Steve at a nearby eatery, right after the driving lessons. After dinner, Tatay and Kuya Nico started to get ready to watch a basketball game at the village plaza which started at nine o'clock that night, blest with perfect weather and cooler breeze from the full moon's radiant light.

The winner of that game will be Kuya Nico's and Liam's team's opponent the following Saturday. That was something to look forward too!

I was about to retire for the night, when I heard a truck brake, stopping at the front of our house, followed by the sound of Liam's footsteps at the door. I was surprised and so happy to see Kuya Steve for I was so thankful of his guidance and help towards Liam! I politely offered him drinks, but Liam was so quick and already on his way to grab him one. I had a feeling that Liam intentionally arranged for Kuya Steve to visit me while Tatay was not around. "Cheeky boy," I smilingly told myself.

Politely, Kuya Steve asked me about my meeting with the Mother Superior and application to the convent. Sadly, I told him all what had transpired in that interview. As usual, he remained quiet and I couldn't gauge what was running through his mind. I thought this was my chance to ask him the questions I've been meaning to ask. "Please God, help me to be strong and bold enough." This was my prayer to help me compose myself.

Tatay had the impression that Kuya Steve was wooing me. Being a man, he knew it, but I absolutely disagreed with him, and confirmed that we were just classmates and friends.

"Now that you've finished your degree and no more homework and projects, may I ask you a direct question with straightforward answer?" was the boldest question I had ever asked! He looked at me in bewilderment, the question took him by surprise. He simply said, "I will do my best."

I asked, "So then, will you still visit me and if so, why?" He was ready to answer when Liam brought the drinks in and interrupted us with his excitement towards his driving test on Monday. As well as the championship games that next Saturday. He happily invited Kuya Steve to attend the games as moral support and of course Liam received a definite yes from him! Cheerfully, Liam went on talking and my question remained unanswered, until Kuya Steve prepared to leave and said that my question will be answered in his next visit.

Two memorable events in Liam's life happened that week. He was over the moon, as he passed the driving test and at the same time, their team won the championship game, with Tatay and Kuya Steve both there to cheer him on. Tatay, overwhelmed with the euphoria of his sons' winning, invited the whole team to have snacks and drinks at our house.

It was indeed a night to remember, where Kuya Nico and Liam as teammates in that team, for the first time won the Championship Title of the Town's Basketball League, which was a valuable and prestigious achievement! I thanked God and fervently prayed that this was the start of their new and blessed life, away from the temptation of drugs and alcohol!

Also, Kuya Steve never got around to answering my question, not until later anyway.

Another year passed, Kuya Steve was now my co-teacher at the college where we both graduated. I sadly left Saint Mary's Academy and I gladly accepted the offer of my 'Alma Mater' to teach high school, whilst also being a part time librarian. Due to its proximity to our house, I readily grabbed the opportunity and enjoyed the convenience of daily short walks to and from the school. At the same time, Liam needed more attention, as sadly he was again in trouble with the police and got locked up for the second time! He got involved in a robbery with his bad peer group and found to be an accomplice to the crime. Tatay completely abandoned him and chose not to go home anymore on weekends so he didn't have to deal with him and also to avoid people's judgement and bitter tongues.

So that Saturday night, I was alone in the big empty house, when Kuya Steve knocked at the door and I joyfully let him in. I was just happy to see him, maybe because of my loneliness and distress with what happened with Liam again. He most probably knew it too. I had to grab that chance to ask him again the question which all this time was left unanswered.

With no hesitancy he simply said, "Don't you know the saying, '**actions speak louder than words**?' You must be the naivest person in the whole world!" "Ouch!" was my reaction.

I remained silent as I recalled Tatay's jealousy and insecurities towards him and that was why! He knew it and I didn't! Stephen was right for calling me a naïve person!

The whole week, I prayed and asked God for guidance what to do with Liam and Tatay's grievously disturbing relationship and for myself too! I was drowning and I desperately needed a rescuer! "God, help me, show me the way how to deal with my troubled brother, who was totally abandoned by Tatay." After my ardent prayers, I instantaneously thought of my Uncle Pablo, who was the town mayor's secretary at the time and bravely paid him a visit. I humbly asked him a big favour to help his nephew and confided in him regarding Tatay's total abandonment of his son. He compassionately said that he will do his best to help him.

After two long weeks in prison, Liam walked out a free man! This time, he must have learnt lessons and hopefully resolved to leave his bad friends and follow the right path in life.

Again, I praised and thanked God for His guidance and surrendered Liam completely to His graces and mercy!

At the college premises, I avoided Stephen. I was not sure what to call him, now that I knew he had this feeling for me… what do you call it? Love? He never said those words to me, but he said, "Actions speak louder than words" Okay, I got it, but I was thinking, why can't it be both? What do you think?

Next day, was 8th of December, the Feast of the Immaculate Conception of the Blessed Virgin Mary, a holyday of obligation of the Catholic Church and a public holiday. As early as 3:30 in the morning, I got ready to attend mass at the cathedral, where annually the feast was being celebrated. I chose the earliest five o'clock mass, to avoid big crowds. As I travelled to the place, I really felt that I needed a man like Stephen mainly to discipline my brother Liam, who was already abandoned by Tatay and at the same time, my rescuer too. I closed my eyes and fervently prayed to God for a SIGN, if HE approves of this man to be my lifetime partner. I deeply contemplated God's plan for me… am I now on another calling?

Am I impelled to be a married woman? I desperately needed guidance from heaven!

Once inside the cathedral, I immediately made my way to my favourite refuge, the quietest and holiest place, which is God's holy sanctuary in the Tabernacle, to give Him my utmost homage and reverence. In Christian traditions, it is the sacrament house in which the Holy Eucharist (consecrated communion hosts) is stored as part of the "reserved sacrament" rite. Silently and fervently, I prayed; and as I surrendered all my burdens to God, I experienced this intense and indescribable feeling, and felt my knees moving towards Mother Mary's image, next to the tabernacle. Then I ardently asked her to intercede in my prayer. I desperately asked God for signs about what to do with my life and rescue me from this feeling of suffocation! With eyes closed, all of a sudden, my heart started throbbing fast, my face turned red, sweat on my forehead and felt prompted by the Holy Spirit to say,

"If ever I would see Stephen anytime today, on this Most Holy and Blessed day, it is a SIGN, that God's plan for me is to be a married woman and approved him to be my spouse."

I stayed in that same position, eyes closed for few more minutes, my sweat and tears flowing freely down my cheeks. I then quickly wiped my face with a white handkerchief. I was in total ecstasy! My body felt weak after that divine intervention, but overwhelmed with love, peace and joy in my heart and whole being! Then I gently stood up when I heard the angelic voices started singing! It was a majestic moment!

The Holy Mass started solemnly with the song for Mary, "Gentle Woman" and I could feel the presence of hundreds of angels singing with the choir as the smell of incense filled the air, and to me, this smelt like heaven!

At the 'Peace be with you' portion of the mass, where you have to greet people beside and around you, I saw the huge cathedral filled with thousands of devotees, there were even some devotees outside the cathedral. The mass celebration ended gloriously with the choir singing the 'Magnificat!'

As I was seated at the front, I stayed for a few minutes, waiting for the people to head out. I sincerely and devotedly continued my prayers and petitions and completely surrendered everything to God to what this special holyday brought to me!

When the traffic inside the church had eased, I stood up and walked towards the main door.

Right there at the door, there was a man gently waving at me! Guess who?

My heart leapt with joy! I had goosebumps all over my body and with tears in my eyes, I thought of my divine conversation with God, the Holy Spirit and Mother Mary just hours ago… and right at that very moment **"THE SIGN"** came to fruition, a lot sooner than expected! I wasn't even out of the door! God is all knowing; He knows the heart's desire of all and certainly, knows best Stephen's pure heart. Without any single doubt in my mind and soul, God clearly affirmed and approved of him to be my spouse! With this sublime feeling, I felt so peaceful in my heart, immensely elated upon reflection on this verse from Psalm 139:1-4,

> *The All-knowing God, "O Lord, you have examined me and you know me. You know when I sit and when I rise; you discern my thoughts from afar. You observe my activities and times of rest; you are familiar with all my ways. Before a word is formed in my mouth, you know it entirely, O Lord."*

As we went out of the cathedral's door, Stephen eagerly invited me to have breakfast in the next suburb's famous restaurant, known for its special menus, that is, if I had no plans for the day. Without too much thought, I accepted his kind invitation!

I couldn't believe that I was seated in the front seat of the director's car!

Being a public holiday, Stephen asked the permission of 'Tatang,' no other than the college director, to use his car. He treated Stephen as his adopted son, after almost ten years of being his trusted driver. In fact, Tatang and his wife 'Ima' used to spray Stephen with cologne before he left their house for his regular Saturday visits to me and made sure, he looked neat and presentable. Later on, I learned from Stephen that this loving couple sincerely and delightfully approved of me to be his future wife. ("Tatang" and "Ima" also mean father and mother in our local dialect) This lovely couple had been acting parents to all the self-supporting students. Although childless, they were reciprocated with lots of love from their beneficiaries and made a lot of difference in their lives of being disadvantaged, Stephen being one of them. Right after the first year of Stephen's stay at the college, Tatang and Ima told him to live with them, much to his surprise and gratitude. That's the reason why Stephen gave his full and genuine service to this remarkable couple, the director and principal of the College, well known philanthropists and his loving foster parents.

Finally, we had reached our destination after all those beautiful recollections while driving!

Stephen chose the corner spot with a square table for four, so we had enough space. As a gentleman, he guided me to the chair where he assigned me to sit and he was about to sit right in front of me. But hastily and bravely, I stopped him and pointed to the seat next to me! Wide-eyed and red-faced Stephen was baffled and asked, "Why, are you sure?"

Maybe, he was thinking that something was wrong with me, as he pondered with shock as to why I acted in such an unusual manner to which he wasn't accustomed to! He reluctantly followed what I suggested and respectfully sat beside me!

Do you want to know more of my unpredictable actions? I bet you do! Well, I nervously took both of his big and rough hands in mine, looked into his bewildered eyes, and with a sweet smile, I boldly uttered these words, **"We are now okay!"**

There you go, I said those words as a sign of my commitment to him! I couldn't believe it myself, as I felt so brave, with no fear at all, but so confident and full of faith that the Holy Spirit gave me the power to be strong and courageous! I had tears in my eyes; tears of joy, happiness and peace! Stephen was also in tears, as he pulled out his white handkerchief to wipe my tears, and his! He gently embraced me, wrapping his strong, muscly arms around me for quite a while, savouring this unexpected momentous event, as both our tears of rapturous joy kept flowing down our cheeks! That was a very precious and holy moment in our lives for we both felt the Holy Spirit hovering over us!

From then on, annually, we faithfully start the day of December 8 with an early morning Holy Mass, followed by a simple breakfast as our "The Sign" anniversary and thanksgiving for God's love and guidance towards us! It divinely marked the momentous day of God's affirmation and approval of this remarkable man as the right spouse for me! Praise God!

> *"Where else could I go from your Spirit? Where could I flee from your presence? You are there if I ascend the heavens; you are there if I descend to the underworld. If I ride on the wings of the dawn and settle on the far side of the sea, even there your hand shall guide me, and your right hand shall hold me safely." (Psalm 139:7-10)*

2. God's Gift of Life

1976

The following year of 1976, we had set our marriage date in April, before Stephen left the country as an overseas worker, in case his application would be successful. Tatay wasn't happy, and even suggested to hold the wedding when Stephen finished his contract after a year. But I insisted and asked the help of my Uncle Pablo to talk to him. I knew that Tatay can't afford to lose me managing our ancestral home, with the thought that I might leave him after marriage. Uncle Pablo eagerly agreed to speak with Tatay to approve our wedding plan in April. He explained to him that he can request us to stay and live with him and my brothers. Tatay finally consented and simple nuptial preparations began. "Oh praise and thank You, Oh Lord God Almighty!"

True to our words, Stephen and I lived with Tatay and my two brothers in our ancestral home. I haven't seen how happy my father was on his usual weekend-homecomings, bringing home lots of foodies and goodies from the city, while proudly explaining what they were and came from, especially when Stephen was around! I thought, it was his way of thanking Stephen for not taking me away from him.

Days and months passed of my being a married woman, I found joy, peace and security in the presence of Stephen. He has always been a man few of words, but a silent achiever.

Christmas of 1976 was our very first Christmas as a big family in the ancestral home. We had decorated the house with the season's trimmings and buntings and a huge bright Christmas tree, stringed around with colourful lights and an angel dressed with a silky-glittery white gown on the very top of it! It was strategically positioned near the wide windows, which the passers-by never missed looking at it with awe!

Tatay gladly brought home from the city lots of foodies and chocolates. This was the first time ever, that we had this very happy, colourful and meaningful Christmas!

On the last week of December, Stephen broke the surprising news that his application for an overseas contract worker was successful. He knew that I wasn't too keen about his plan. He justified his decision saying that his meagre income as a teacher will not be enough to fulfill our dream of securing our own house and support the future of our family, anticipating the time when we will be blest with children.

That night, I was restless and unhappy about Stephen's initial plan of being an overseas worker without telling me and most importantly asking God's signs of approval. He mentioned this to me, after he sent his application papers. He noticed my tossing and turning as well as my heavy sighs. He stood up and brought me a warm glass of milk. Then he held my hands and said, "I am so sorry if I haven't told you about the application. It all happened so quick on one day. The recruiter was efficient, we were just asked to sign the papers and all was done. All we had to do was to wait for the result. I had to grab every opportunity for our future's sake. I hope you understand me as the family's provider and bread winner." His gentle words had touched me and felt peaceful about it. But I'd asked the question, "Had you prayed for it and asked God's sign of approval?" He looked at me and replied, "Yes, I had! God is a loving God and understands me." I accepted that reply, cuddled in his warm arms, and slept peacefully.

When I woke up in the morning, I was dizzy and felt like vomiting. It seemed that I didn't have the energy to go to school, so I asked Stephen to tell the principal that I don't feel well.

He went to teach only his three classes in the morning and at lunch time, he arrived home driving Tatang's car, with the intention of taking me to the doctor to be checked. After the check up and had filled up the questionnaire, the doctor said, "I think, you are pregnant! But we will find out one hundred percent tomorrow as soon I received your urine test result."

Deep in my heart, I knew that I have God's gift of life within me!

God is always faithful to His promises. The much-awaited result of my check-up turned to be positive. I was pregnant to our first child. Praise God Almighty!

This Christmas of 1976, Stephen and I received the greatest gifts ever…this precious gift of a child and was seconded by the successful application of Stephen as an overseas contract worker! Thank You, Lord God for these precious and cherished gifts to us!

As soon as Tatay learned about the good news, he went shopping for celebration! He told me to invite his elder brother Uncle Pablo and family next door, while he cheerfully prepared and proudly cooked his specialty dishes. After our delicious and sumptuous lunch, Tatay raised his glass of wine for a toast of thanksgiving! I think this was the happiest moment in his life! I felt his extreme joy and overwhelming happiness to be a grandfather soon, as he eagerly announced the good news to all of his siblings and close friends!

3. Stephen's Greener Pasture

In March 1977, the whole household - Tatay, my two brothers and young Jade accompanied me to the airport to wish Stephen a safe journey and God's blessings. I did not like, nor have I ever liked goodbyes! Though heartbroken, I had to see Stephen go, kissed him goodbye and say "till we meet again." I couldn't control my tears as I watched the plane take off, until it just vanished out of sight. I gently stroked my three-month pregnant tummy and his words were still ringing in my ears when he said, "Take extra care of yourself and our baby, my dearest. I am always with you in spirit and prayers." I confidently said to myself, "Yes, I will and I have no fear for God is with me!"

Days and months quickly passed and I was very thankful for the library's new project and coaching sessions for my students for the forthcoming oratorical contest, for these kept me busy enough to flittingly forget my loneliness of missing Stephen's presence.

My monthly pregnancy check-ups went smoothly. On my fifth month of pregnancy, unexpectedly the obstetrician asked me if I wanted to know my child's gender. It was a quick negative answer, as I wanted to share the joy of waiting with Stephen until the delivery day of our first born.

What I fervently prayed to God was to find a reliable woman as my house keeper and support after child birth. This was the time when I missed and longed for my Nanay and Aunt Nina, who were already both gone to their eternal home in heaven.

That night, I dreamt of a room with a baby crib inside adorned with white laces on its handle and a pink blanket with tiny white pillows. There was an old woman putting things in order!

I was in awe when I woke up, thanking and praising God for I knew and felt that He spoke to me conveying His message, "Be still and know that I am your God." (Psalm 46:10)

From then on, I felt so secured and peaceful, looking forward to dream again and listen to God's message.

Two months before my delivery due date, Aunt Encar visited me and happily broke the good news that her former housemaid was looking for work and mentioned my need for one. She told her to come and see me. The next day, a mature-gentle looking lady knocked at the door with two bags of clothes as if I knew her from somewhere long time ago! That cherished moment was the beginning of having a reliable and kind companion at home.

"Thank you, Lord!"

With deep expectant faith and confidence, I was ready to be a mother and father at the same time, in the temporary absence of Stephen. I took great assurance in the faith that God is with me always!

September 25, 1977, at two o'clock in the morning, I felt signs of labour contractions, so, I woke Aunt Lyla up, who had been sleeping in my room upon my request. She immediately got up and alarmed my two brothers to organise transport to take me to the hospital.

Five hours later, as the sun radiated its glorious rays, a beautiful, gorgeous and healthy baby girl was born! I requested Kuya Nico and Liam to send Stephen an express telegram informing him this great news! Praise God Almighty!

I enjoyed looking after Jasmine, a healthy and bubbly baby with the kind assistance of Aunt Lyla who really showed me her expertise in bathing and dressing babies. I learned a lot from her different experiences, including herbal medications as emergency applications in the absence of doctor's prescriptions. I deeply appreciated her presence in my life!

Day by day, God really manifested His constant Divine protection, especially on that day when Jasmine fell down the stairs! She was eleven months old and loved being on her walker, jumping and walking around in the spacious lounge room. She seemed to be singing along and dancing, while Tatay's music was on at full blast. When all of a sudden, I felt my heart leap out of my chest and I envisioned a frightening scene in my mind like in a movie of Jasmine rolling and falling down the stairs of approximately twelve steps down to the ground floor. I instinctively yelled out, "Check on Jasmine! The door might be open and she might go out to the porch!" I hastily ran to the door, at the same time, I was calling all the angels and saints to save Jasmine. I hadn't even finished yelling out my words, when I heard the sound of the walker from the porch falling down the stairs! I saw Jasmine at the bottom of the stairs, smiling and waving her toy at me, as if saying, "That was a wonderful trip!" She came out of that fall unscathed! Oh my God, and all angels and saints, thank you for saving my baby and holding her in the palm of your hands!

4. Homecoming: The Prize of a Family Being Together

1978

Tatay ordered a whole roasted pig as one of the major menus for Jasmine's first year birthday celebration. This was a customary tradition for first born baby in the family, and most especially Tatay's first grandchild! The backyard was decorated with buntings and colourful banners, with decorated tables and chairs and a specific long buffet table covered with freshly washed banana leaves filled with different kinds of traditional dishes, desserts and drinks, an allotted space for the whole roasted pig in the middle! It was indeed like a town fiesta! I invited our parish priest for prayers and blessing before the meal.

Everyone enjoyed the food cooked by my Aunties and some friends as they proudly explained how they cooked their specialty dishes, as if it was a Master Class Chefs' competition. The children were busy with their variety of games organised by Jade and Liam and most of all, were excited with their give-away toys courtesy of Tatay, which he bought in Manila. It was indeed a long tiring day, but full of fun, where in everyone enjoyed the food and games, especially Jasmine, who fell asleep by herself! She must have been very tired!

But one thing for sure, we all missed the presence of Stephen and at the same time felt so sorry for him for having missed this very special occasion of our first child's first birthday celebration! Liam volunteered to take lots of photos to be sent to him as soon as possible!

At the end of the month, I was back to teaching after my one-year maternity leave.

Jasmine was already trained drinking milk directly from a glass, because she didn't like the feel and the taste of the milk bottle's rubber teat. This made it very convenient for Aunt Lyla during her meal times. Boiled and mashed potatoes, soft boiled rice and soup and other foods expertly prepared and taught by Aunt Lyla, were already introduced to her. I trusted Aunt Lyla's expertise on certain foods recommended for the child's age.

I did look forward for Stephen's arrival the next year. By March, his contract would be finished and would be required to go home and renew another one, if he chose to.

Jasmine showed a lot of progress with her normal child development in all aspects, most especially with her social and communication skills. At one year and four months, she could easily say a full sentence, though some words were incomplete, but comprehensible. She became the favourite baby in our small village. Women and children would stop by to play with her, when Aunt Lyla walked her around the park for morning sunshine.

One afternoon, a yellow cab stopped in front of our house and a dark bearded man in a denim jacket, stepped out of the car, picked up the rest of his luggage and hurriedly went up the stairs! Oh my God, Stephen finally came home safely! Praise God! At first, I wasn't able to recognise him, not until I glanced at his luggage and saw his familiar speedy movements. I quickly picked up Jasmine, who was busy playing in the lounge room, rushed to the front door and welcomed him with a warm loving kiss and a very tight hug and introduced him gently to Jasmine. She was shy and a bit scared of this unfamiliar bearded man, which was a normal reaction. In Stephen's excitement to present his gift to Jasmine, he showed her this big walking doll as tall as her, which only hand carried on the plane like a fragile gift! As he put the doll down and switched it on, it started walking and talking saying, "Hi, my name is Jasmine." Oh, my goodness! Jasmine took one look and shocked, she cried loudly, so scared of the doll, holding on to me tightly and hid her face! I told Stephen to settle down first and win her later through goodies like other toys and chocolates that he brought home.

I saw his face go red with disappointment as he frustratedly packed the walking doll into its original packaging. He said that he totally understood Jasmine's feelings and reactions.

After dinner, Jasmine was ready to go to bed and kissed everyone good night. Young children's feelings generally are transient. So, this time she eagerly kissed her father and uttered the sweetest word 'Papa!' He was in tears upon hearing that word, as Jasmine quickly fell asleep because she missed her afternoon nap.

Stephen was quite emotional and admitted the pain of being away from home and family. He was tortured when he learned about Jasmine falling down the stairs and couldn't get over the feeling of guilt of his absence during those times when he was most needed. He didn't like it at all! He told me firmly that he had decided not to renew his contract to work overseas and that he would never leave us till the end of time! He said, "God just let me have a taste of being away from loved ones, so I will see the prize of this precious treasure of being together as a family." Then, we prayed together praising and thanking the Lord for His love and faithfulness to us! "Never again I'll be away from you and my children as long as I breathe!", he vowed.

Early one morning, Stephen took Jasmine with him to the park, to play, walk around and enjoy the morning sunshine. He securely sat Jasmine on the swing, gently pushed her and could see her thrill and excitement as she continuously giggled and even asked him to push her higher and higher!

That day was the oratorical competition to be held at three o'clock in the afternoon at the main hall. After lunch, I went to see my student-contestant and gave her my final suggestions and encouragement. I was satisfied with her performance and confident that she will win a place. When we walked out of the room, I saw Tatang, the director and gladly, gave me the good news that Stephen was offered a position to teach again! Tatang confided that after two days upon Stephen's arrival, he eagerly submitted his application to teach again and told him his firm decision never to leave us anymore. This great news made me run up and hug Tatang for giving him another opportunity to use his hard-earned education and talent. So now, aside from being a teacher during the day, he will be a driver at night! What a hardworking man! Stephen really looked after our future and aimed to save money to buy a piece of land for our dream house.

We thank you Lord God, for all your blessings and graces to our family!

Chapter 4

Our Family Is Getting Bigger

"You did not choose me; it was I who chose you and sent you to go and bear much fruit, fruit that will last. And everything that you ask the Father in my Name, He will give you." (John 15:16)

1. Three Angels from Heaven

1981

Within five years of God's graces and blessings, Stephen and I were blessed with three beautiful children. After Jasmine, Matthew was born, and then Lily, the youngest and the last. We have three angels from heaven! I gave birth to Jasmine at the hospital, being the first baby. But with Matthew and Lily, I found it comfortable and peaceful at home, with my close friend as my midwife, who was also Jasmine's godmother. It was a great joy when we were blessed with the second child being a boy, as the surname keeper in the family. It's our tradition that the male baby maintains the family's name, that's why some parents name their baby boy after the father's name. With us we named Matthew after the saint of the day when he was born. Stephen and I had agreed to name our children this way with the firm belief that the saint constantly looks after them and protects them from any harm and danger. Again, for the third time, God blessed us with another beautiful angel baby girl Lily, born safely and peacefully at home. Alarmingly, I bled profusely which made me really nervous and scared as I thought of Nanay who died at 28 years old due to internal bleeding from a miscarriage. My midwife said that if after an hour, the bleeding did not stop, then we had to go to the hospital. Thank God, the bleeding stopped, until I felt normal again. As soon as Stephen arrived from the city, he gently kissed me and said, "This angel baby girl is our last! Praise God for saving and protecting you and our angel baby Lily from any endangerment and peril!"

The ancestral household became bigger and bigger, especially when Kuya Nico's wife Norma gave birth with their second child too. They had one girl, as the eldest and one boy, the youngest. Having five little children in the house, shouting and running around, was a bit chaotic, yet we were all happy together as one big family!

A very memorable event was scheduled that coming Friday, so I requested Stephen to finish work early, so he could attend that momentous occasion. Finally, I'd finished my Master's Degree in Education! He was so proud of me with all my sacrifices of teaching in two schools, and for this reason he had to equal my efforts by working two jobs too. I think that is a man's ego to be the "main breadwinner", which is natural. But I kept reminding him, that this is not a competition, but rather, a team-work for the bright future of our beloved family. He humbly apologised and admitted his silliness. My passion to learn more, pushed me to pursue my education further and I reaped the rewards of being offered a position as a college professor in the neighbouring town, even if I hadn't officially finished my master's degree yet. I gladly accepted the rare opportunity.

Aunt Lyla sadly broke the news to us, that her children were coming to pick her up.

Her very ill husband requested to see her for reconciliation before he dies. He was given few months to live by the doctor. Aunt Lyla and her husband separated long time ago due to his womanising ways and multiple affairs. Her life's story bonded us together due to similarities of our family experiences.

My own father got married for the second time, but after two years, Nanay Julie, my stepmother decided to leave him due to his infidelity as well as his drunkenness. Jade, their daughter was only two years old then, and when she had reached her school age, she had stayed with us upon my request. For this reason, Aunt Lyla and I became really close to each other like a real Aunt or even a mother to me!

It was a big blow to us losing Aunt Lyla, who stayed faithfully with me day in and day out, for almost six years. Truly, she was God's answer to my prayers of having someone to support me! After our hugs and kisses, I couldn't control my tears, when it was time for her to go with her children and I remember thinking that maybe I wouldn't see her anymore.

Really, I didn't like goodbyes!

We needed someone to replace Aunt Lyla. I knew that she wouldn't be easily replaced in terms of her expertise, but because the children were already bigger at this time, we only needed some help with looking after them, having someone there to accompany them during those specific times when Stephen and I were at our day time classes at the college.

Again, God manifested His love by giving us His wisdom and guidance. I had learned that my younger first cousin Bella, who just finished high school, wanted to pursue her education, but her parents were unable to afford her school fees in college. Stephen and I immediately went to visit her family and offered our help to sponsor her college education. Her parents happily accepted the generous offer! So, from then on, Bella stayed with us and helped us in return by looking after the children in the afternoon until Stephen arrived from his teaching, then she would go to college for her night classes. That was indeed a perfect arrangement through the guidance of the Holy Spirit! Thank You, Oh Lord God Almighty!

2. We Have to Go

1984

Days and months went by so fast. Both Stephen and I were busy with our professions as teachers during the day. Until I was given another blessing of teaching at night as a college professor in a nearby town, and at the same, Stephen worked as a driver too. This time we needed another helper to look after the children when Bella left for her night classes. Through God's graces and blessings, we were able to have Stephen's two nieces, Sen and Rosie, look after the children when we were both out at night, with the same privilege of Bella's free education. We offered to sponsor their high school education, which was delightfully accepted by their parents. Their mother Alice is Stephen's elder sister! God is good, all the time! Everything worked out well!

Stephen and I both enjoyed our jobs during the week, but always looked forward to the weekends to spend quality time with our big family. Tatay, a healthy and energetic grandfather of five grandchildren, as well as a very busy truck broker in the city, also enthusiastically looked forward for the weekends to play with his cheeky and gorgeous grandchildren!

Kuya Nico's family also stayed with us, as well as Liam with 'one kitchen,' which meant whatever food was cooked in the kitchen was for everyone in the household. Kuya Nico's job was on and off. There were times that he was found drinking with his friends, living like a single man without a family. I remembered the time when I overheard Kuya Nico and his wife Norma arguing and fighting over his drunkenness and my sister-in-law's jealousy over another woman! During those times, I sensed the mess in their marriage. Their issues became the catalyst for Stephen to think about separating from the big household, due to the open domestic disputes often heard inside the house even with the presence of children! I hesitated at the idea because of our promise to Tatay, but Stephen explained the importance of our children's welfare more than anything else in the world! He didn't want the children to grow up in that kind of environment. He believed that more than ten years of our stay at the ancestral home was a reflection of one's loyalty to his promise and the reason for separation was acceptable and reasonable enough.

That weekend, Stephen was ready to tell Tatay about our plan of leaving. I ardently prayed and humbly asked God to touch Tatay with the gift of understanding towards our decision.

Truly, God is good! Tatay understood every single word that Stephen told him and he even said that he will go home straight to our abode on weekends, rather than to the ancestral home! Of course, we overwhelmingly welcomed him with open arms! Praise God!

3. Stephen's New Business Venture

Everything went smoothly with our planned strategic move of leaving the ancestral home scheduled the next month. I did feel the pain of sadness as I thought of leaving my beloved home of birth, but the call of my loyalty towards my husband and own family was at stake and opted not to risk it. We openly told the whole household what our plans were, to move out and pursue Stephen's new business venture which was animal husbandry. To be granted a permit with that kind of business, a spacious backyard was an essential requirement. It was a valid reason, since he was serious about it, and at the same time a good reason to avoid hurting or offending anyone, which might have caused misunderstanding in the family.

Before we left that weekend, Tatay organised a little feast called "despedida" in Spanish, which means a "leaving party." He invited his brother and family next door, just to send us off in a joyful mood, though I could sense sadness and gloominess in the air. I kept telling and assuring everyone that we were just a stone's throw away, in the next village!

That semestral break, was spent busily cleaning and arranging everything in the proper order I planned for in our new two-storey house, which was a little bit smaller than our ancestral house, but which had a big, spacious backyard with an added bonus of an old shack ready for the piglet which Stephen's friend Elliot planned to drop off the following day. The children were all excited and couldn't wait to see and touch the piglet, as that would have been their first time to see one. That night, when we all prayed the rosary and said our individual prayers, we were surprised to hear one of the children pray for the safe arrival of the piglet to our house! Stephen and I looked at each other with pride in our hearts for having such good and sensible children!

Praise God for blessing us with good, angel-like children!

The next day was a Saturday, which meant that Tatay will be around in the afternoon and by that time, Elliot would have dropped the piglet off. The kids were motivated to help with tidying up the whole house, with Bella giving them instructions with where everything was to go and what needed to be done. Stephen had a good deal with Elliot. He gave him the female piglet for free to look after her until such time she will be ready to be a mother pig, in which time he will drop off the male pig for reproduction. Once she got pregnant and had piglets, Stephen would simply return to Elliot one piglet of his choice, whether male or female. What a perfect and kind arrangement! Since then, Elliot became one of Stephen's closest and trusted friend to this day!

The children always looked forward to the afternoons when they arrived from school, to spray and clean Becky, the name they eagerly gave the piglet as soon as they saw her. The more they got excited when they heard the good news that it wouldn't be long until Becky became a mother pig! One afternoon, Stephen reminded the children to be very gentle with her, because very soon she will be Mother Becky and will have little piglets of her own.

Until midnight one night, Stephen and I stayed awake to keep an eye on Becky, while the kids were upstairs soundly asleep.

The next morning, everyone gathered around the shack, happily watching Becky and her fifteen cute, pinkish and healthy piglets! We were all surprised by the numbers of piglets she'd delivered! Elliot said, based on his experience, Becky will be a very good mother, and genetically had a great and healthy pig's reproductive system. True enough, we found Becky really gentle with her fifteen piglets. She would lie down slowly to make sure she wouldn't hurt any one of the piglets. She was extremely patient when two piglets would fight over one nipple, as there weren't enough nipples for fifteen piglets. She only had fourteen nipples and for fifteen piglets, it was a big challenge for poor Becky! Which is why Stephen always patiently stayed around during the piglets' feeding time to assist her.

I noticed too how Tatay loved his weekend-homecomings at our house. Not only did he enjoy being with his grandchildren, he also loved watching the fifteen piglets that grew up too quickly, especially as he only saw them on a weekly basis. He was totally amazed too with Stephen's expertise with handling the new venture. After forty days, the piglets would be ready to be sold, before Becky's milk ran dry. Each piglet was quickly sold until all fourteen were gone, which saddened the whole family, because we all missed them, as they quickly became a part of our big family.

Elliot visited us one afternoon, to pick up the last piglet of his choice and happily brought with him a bottle of wine to celebrate one round of Becky's successful reproductive mission, as well as Stephen's gained expertise with his new business venture. Oh! and to his surprise, he unexpectedly earned a huge amount of money from those fourteen piglets! Praise God!

Chapter 5

The Value of Spirituality in One's Life

"If you have received Christ Jesus as Lord, continue to live in Him. Be rooted and built up in Him, strengthened in the faith as you were taught, and overflowing with thankfulness." (Colossians 2:6-7)

1. A Family that Prays Together, Stays Together

1986

With our ten years of marriage, Stephen and I remained faithful to our promises to God to keep our family in order and gradually but firmly imprint in our children the love of God and the importance of praying to Him every day. Praying the rosary at night before bed was a set pattern in our everyday life. The solemnity of Sundays as a day for church and family bonding was instilled in their young minds and became a meaningful family weekend routine.

The children enthusiastically looked forward to Sundays, as they found it a day of relaxation, free day and play day! A family that prays together, plays together, certainly stays together!

I clearly remembered those Sundays, that right after mass, we leisurely walked to the local shop in the neighbourhood to buy two dollars' worth of hot chips securely wrapped with the butcher's paper, which ended up as a huge bundle enough to occupy the whole dining table.

We enjoyed eating the hot chips as we dipped them in tomato sauce, while we read the Sunday papers that the news boy, delivered weekly to our porch where we left him there, a fifty-cent coin the night before. The Sunday newspaper was divided into five sections:

Headline news, sports, holidays, entertainment, and puzzles. We had our favourite sections, then we all swapped around until we each had read the whole lot and exchanged our ideas and thoughts. What a simple life during those olden days, as I reflect in today's world, especially with modern technology! I'm sure you can imagine and might even agree with me, that what I've shared would be a far different scene to what a Sunday these days would look like.

There's no more that joy of sitting together reading the newspaper, because modern technology has taken over; for nowadays, the news is easily accessible on mobile phones!

You can imagine each child very busy playing their own modern gadgets or the teenagers on Skype or FaceTime with their friends and parents maybe in the gym or in the garden or even maybe away for a weekend conference or getaway. I can see that in today's world, the number one factor in family's breakdown is communication due to the highly evolving technology with gadgets which have sadly and dramatically cut down personal interactions.

But having said that, I'm sure, there are still some families out there, who still firmly believe in the importance of a Sunday family gatherings; a time to sit down and update on the past week's experiences whether good or bad; a time for God and family bonding together in love and unity!

On a fortnightly basis, Sundays were also a day of visiting Stephen's parents, which the children eagerly waited for as they really enjoyed visiting their grandparents, as well as the thrill of seeing and touching the different farm animals, which they didn't see in town. That set pattern was of significant value, because the children learned the ways of life, living on a farm, aside from the enormous love and affection they had experienced from their grandparents, to which I'm sure enhanced their growth and development emotionally and socially. They'd learned the value of politeness, respect, love and care for the elderly.

Acquiring these values are factors which will surely influence the good and appropriate behaviour of children mentally, emotionally and socially as they grew up into adulthood.

Indeed, it is really important to spend quality time with the family on Sundays and start the day with God, through the Holy Mass. This develops the strong faith and love for God and eventually becomes a habit of calling and asking God's help towards their little and simple needs. After the religious obligation, the next routine was relaxation and fun with the children, like playing cricket in the backyard or ride their bikes around the neighbourhood or just simply watch shows or movies together, while munching on snacks such as popcorn, nuts and chips. These were some of our children's cherished memories which all factored in awarding positive effects on their character, personality and whole being.

Stephen and I implanted into our children's hearts and minds the great value of putting God first as number one priority in their lives.

> *"Set your heart first on the kingdom of God and His justice and these things will also be given to you." (Matthew 6:33)*

2. Our Spiritual Life as a Couple

The "three persons in a marriage" formula has been our mantra throughout our married life, since we attended the pre-nuptial seminar until this present time. "This is the formula for a successful marriage," as explained to us by Fr. Ambo. I asked the question at that time, "Why three?" The priest quickly answered that God must be in the centre of this marriage, because God is love. "Pray to God together, serve God together and stay together in love for God," was his concluding statement during the seminar, which Stephen and I both faithfully kept in our hearts and minds.

Together as a couple, Stephen and I shared and served together the same faith all through the years since the day we got married. Indeed, we both realised and felt, that we get closer every day. Everything must be focused on God's love and goodness as well as each other's emotions and feelings. The key word is love, for this magic word resulted in all of these elements of a successful marriage: respect, trust, gentleness, humility and self-sacrifice.

Now that we had reached our ten years anniversary, I affirm and agree that all of these elements from the mother word LOVE, will lead to a blissful marriage.

Together, we served during the Sunday masses; Stephen as an Acolyte or Minister of the Altar and I, as a reader in the

Liturgy of the Word. Indeed, serving the Lord together as a couple, gave us great feelings of joy and peace!

We felt that Sunday mass attendance and service weren't enough to serve the Lord and repay all His goodness to us. Stephen and I had volunteered to serve as facilitators at parish retreats and recollections scheduled in remote villages, a mission by the diocese held twice a year with the main goal of: Evangelisation, aiming to invite people to know, love and serve God. We'd knocked on doors or spoke to people giving them information on the forthcoming retreats; encouraged and invited them to attend the very important spiritual events in the parish. We'd helped in soliciting food and miscellaneous items to sponsor the weekends activities, for these were offered to people for free. At this point of asking donations to people, whether in cash or in kinds, I discovered the truth behind the famous Bible verse from Matthew 19:24, which says, "Yes, believe me: it is easier for a camel to go through the eye of a needle than for a rich man to enter into the kingdom of heaven."

The poor had expressed their generosity and full support by donating whatever they had in their homes like rice, fruits and vegetables, which helped a lot in the food planning of the kitchen committee. When I had approached the rich, they asked so many questions as if doubting the validity of the mission. In one occasion, I'd pressed the intercom's buzzer of a three-storey-mansion-like property owned by one of the wealthiest men in town and he gave me the smallest jar of coins he'd kept. I was in total shock and was instantaneously reminded of this scriptural verse!

Much to our joy in doing this from Friday night until Sunday around noon time, we were worried about Bella who was left alone looking after the three kids. God answered our prayers and sent us two nieces from Stephen's family this time to support Bella, with the same arrangement of giving them free education in exchange of looking after the children and household chores. Indeed, we'd immersed ourselves in our service to God.

We both witnessed God's affirmation of our humble service, through His mysterious ways of divine providence. God knows all our heart's desire and makes everything possible. We felt humbled and honoured to be instruments in leading people towards God's kingdom.

Oh, praise and thank you Lord God Almighty!

3. My Personal Spirituality

Since the time I lost my mother at almost seven years old, I became so close to God and Mother Mary. During Nanay's funeral, the Mother Superior of the convent where I and Kuya Nico were studying said, "My child, don't be sad; don't be afraid, for you have the Heavenly Mother Mary who will look after you and her Son, Jesus who will be with you always."

These were the words in scripted in my mind, heart and soul, and became my comfort and guide, from then on.

I attended daily mass and enjoyed cleaning the church, as well as arranging flowers at the altar. Later on, at fourteen I joined the Legion of Mary, a lay Catholic organisation whose members give service to the church on a voluntary basis, like visiting the sick in the hospitals, volunteering to do childminding so parents could attend mass as well as cleaning the church. Being an active member of this organisation, made me closer to God and I developed a deeper relationship with Jesus. I loved days spent in reflections and time of conversation with God like a loving Father and friend. Through my regular mass attendance and prayers, I found myself stronger and firmer when the trials and storms of life came. I realised that life would not be complete without the blows and storms of life. The victory of overcoming challenges is the prize of one's strong faith and trust in God's love and faithfulness to His people!

At the age of twenty-two, I discovered my presence of prophetic gifts of dreams and visions.

This was when I was pregnant with our first child Jasmine. My obstetrician asked me if I wanted to know the gender of my baby. It was a quick negative answer, because I wanted to share the joy of waiting with Stephen, who was away as contractual overseas worker at that time. That night, I fervently prayed for a helper who can be my house maid after my child birth. I asked God for a mature lady, as I missed and longed for my mother to give me advice on pregnancy, child birth, raising up children and life in general.

That night I dreamt of a room with a beautiful crib adorned with white laces on its handle, a pink blanket and tiny white pillows. There was an old woman putting everything in order in the room! I woke up in awe, praising and thanking God, because I felt and knew that I have an angel baby girl within me and a mature woman on the way! Praise You, Oh Lord God!

Indeed, all of these came into fruition! Jasmine was born and God sent Aunt Lyla, who faithfully stayed with us for almost six years, as a loving and trusted companion like a real Aunt to me!

From then on, I kept recalling my dreams and started to write them down, with the aim of someday, I will be able to proclaim to the whole world God's unconditional love and faithfulness to His people through dreams and visions. God conveys His message and instructions through these divine channels.

> *"I bless you Lord who is my counsellor;*
> *even at night guides me." (Psalm 16:17)*

> *"Let us consider how we may spur one another*
> *to love and do good works. Do not abandon*
> *the assemblies as some of you do, but encourage*
> *one another, and all the more since the day*
> *is drawing near." (Hebrews 10:24-25)*

Chapter 6

God Works in Mysterious Ways

"Rejoice in the Lord always. I say it again, rejoice; and may everyone experience your gentle and understanding heart. The Lord is near; do not be anxious about anything. In everything resort to prayer and supplication together with thanksgiving and bring your request before God. Then the peace of God, which surpasses all understanding, will keep your hearts and minds in Christ Jesus." (Phil 4:4-7)

1. Migration Opportunity

March 1986

Such a small world! This is a very common saying when something unusual occurred without expectations at all.

Leni, my former high school classmate and best friend became my sister-in-law, being Stephen's younger sister! She studied in the city after our high school graduation and there met Anthony, who later became husband, a programmer-analyst by profession.

Anthony found the rare opportunity of a greener pasture in Australia in 1980. That was the time when Australia opened family migration to men and women with qualifications in nursing and computer programming. Anthony's skill and qualifications, easily paved the way for their migration, with their only two-year old daughter Krissy.

After five long years of hardship and perseverance as migrants of this new world of opportunity, Leni and her husband Anthony became stable financially. Her husband's good earning job as computer analyst and her own full-time job opened the opportunities to secure their own house, send their only daughter to a private school and buy all the comfort of life can offer. They succeeded in achieving their dreams as they explored the new horizon of migrating to this beautiful country!

Looking back to where they came from, Leni and Anthony unselfishly and lovingly thought of their own respective families in the Philippines, and aimed to share with them this financial stability and comfort, they were experiencing and enjoying. They decided to get some sponsorship forms from the Australian embassy with the intention of giving them out to their siblings, when they went back to the Philippines in 1986 with the clear vision and hope that they too would taste the same blessings they had received.

True to their genuine intention, they enthusiastically looked forward to be back home in their motherland. They prepared all their passports, visas and waited for the airplane tickets to be issued to them. So, in March 1986, they safely landed in Manila after long six years and no wonder they all had these nostalgic and ecstatic feelings to be back home!

Stephen's older brother broke the great news that Leni's family will be arriving that coming Saturday morning and will stay in the city with Anthony's family. Then the following day, Sunday they will travel to the province to visit us! We all jumped with joy and excitement, especially myself! I suddenly remembered Leni as a very lonely and sombre girl, and with this change of lifestyle, I envisioned her to be a totally different person as a jovial and fulfilled woman of success. Truly her life story is a model in the wheel of life's triumphant stories!

The much-awaited moment of reunion, after so many years of separation finally came into fruition, when a lovely family of three knocked at our door! With cheers and tears of joy, we jubilantly welcomed lovely Leni, Anthony and gorgeous daughter Krissy with hugs and kisses! We guided them to a long table of "welcome feast of food" brought by the other siblings, turning out to be like a real fiesta. The long table was underlined with freshly washed banana leaves, then arranged with different delicious Spanish, Chinese and native dishes, steamed and grilled fish and lots of steamed vegetables like eggplant, okra, and bitter melon. At the end of the table were assorted desserts like, cassava cake, leche flan, and 'stained glass gelatin' commonly known as cathedral gelatin, proudly cooked and baked by each sibling and on the ground were two eskies filled with cold drinks and ice! As usual, before meals, Stephen led the prayer of thanksgiving especially at this special occasion and everyone shed tears of joy. It was indeed such a joyful and festive reunion!

After our sumptuous lunch, we all went at the front side of the house, sat under the shade of a half-century-old acacia tree and enjoyed the cool breeze and the lovely company of each other. With wide eyes and opened ears, we enthusiastically listened to Leni's and Anthony's interesting stories and experiences, as well as the intensive information on Australia about its climate and weather, education, geography, literacy, employment and most of all, the vast job opportunities of a better future for the family. I was in awe with the big difference of these two countries' way of life and standard of living!

Then, the couple happily stood up and showed us several signed application forms for migration from the Australia embassy. They proudly distributed the forms to each family, who may be interested and eligible to go to Australia! We were all thankful for this act of kindness and thoughtfulness for thinking of us and sharing this big opportunity of a better life. It was like winning a lottery!

The following day, Monday, Leni's family were to travel back to Manila and stay with Anthony's side of family for another two days and then will fly back to Australia. With excitement and eagerness in his heart, Stephen immediately checked the required documents and found out that we have all the complete list of requirements! He joyfully told his sister that we were ready to lodge our application form and kindly requested her to accompany us to the embassy. She then, reviewed the check list of the required documents and she was so delighted to know that we'd completed and passed all the requirements!

Praise God!

2. Dilemma: My Father's Illness

*I*n our regular family prayers, we always acknowledge God's love and goodness to us. We were blessed with enough food on the table, roof over our heads, healthy children in school, enough earnings to buy our daily needs and had the privilege of supporting our nieces for their education. Liam too stayed with us whenever he got lonely at our ancestral home and Tatay faithfully went home to us on weekends. With Stephen's discovery of Becky's second pregnancy, again filled our hearts with joy and thanksgiving for God's bountiful blessings.

On Sundays, after church, we all looked forward to taste the delicious food which Tatay brought home regularly from the city! He kept saying, "Here kiddies, taste the food of Manila!" He was so proud to share with us anything he could especially doting on his grandchildren and found joy being with us even if it was only on weekends.

Everything was going smoothly in our happy household, when unexpectedly during the week, Tatay went home, accompanied by his work mate. He was not feeling well and his supervisor took him to the company's doctor with the recommendation of seeing a specialist. Being sixty years old, a chain smoker and alcohol lover, I felt that Tatay might have heart and lung issues. Stephen and I immediately took emergency leave and thankfully, on the same day was able to secure an appointment with a specialist. The hospital's specialist had a look at the referral letter and said that Tatay had to stay for at least three to four days in the hospital for a thorough check of all his health issues. With hope in our heart, we agreed and left him with prayers for healing and total surrender to God's grace and mercy.

Our migration sponsorship form was successfully lodged with the assistance and kindness of Leni and Anthony. They wished us all the best for the good results and we sincerely thanked them for that opportunity of a lifetime. As we parted ways, once again I lovingly hugged and kissed my best friend Leni, who perfectly showed her loyalty as a true friend and generous sister-in-law! She said, "I would love to see you soon in Australia!" Amen!

That night's family prayer was so emotional, because of Tatay's serious health situation. He was brought home from the hospital, after our family and my sibling's decision not to undergo any more operations or chemotherapy after all the intensive explanations and options given to us by the specialist. He was diagnosed with stage four lung cancer, which had spread to other organs or parts of his body! The specialist advised us to just give him the best food and comfort of peace and happiness being with his loved ones.

I cried out to God! Lord Almighty! You know what is in my heart. I really do feel this pain and anguish of being torn with this dilemma of my family's migration and leaving my sick father!

You know deep in my heart that I can't leave my father in this situation. Heavenly Father, I am tired and totally surrender everything to Your Most Holy Will. Amen! This was my prayer.

3. Medical Check-up Mix up

I sensed deeply Liam's sadness and anxiety, which I could totally understand. He was absolutely devastated with Tatay's sudden illness, at the same time anxious about our plan of migrating to another country. This meant a lot to him: losing my presence as his elder sister, whom he treated more like his mother rather than a sister, which was reciprocated. I lovingly called him, so we could talk seriously with how to face all these challenges ahead of us.

Firstly, I told him how proud I was to know that he was offered to be a delivery driver of a prestigious company in town and most of all, he was like a new person, free from drugs and alcohol. I asked him to remain this way and God will lead him to the best in life!

He had tears in his eyes and hugged me!

Secondly, I mentioned Tatay's illness, that I will never leave him in this condition. I prayed and totally surrendered Tatay to God's will. With full trust in Him, things will fall into place.

Thirdly, I asked him if he had a girlfriend and asked if he was serious about her. I pointed out the value and importance of having a family before, if ever, we leave him. I wanted him to be emotionally settled and happy, so he could focus on his new family, as well as all the good things in life!

He smiled and I think he totally agreed, as I saw the affirmation in his eyes! Praise God!

When we lodged our application in March 1986, one of the questions commonly asked, according to the interviewer was, "How long will it take the whole process till we get the golden price - the visa." The friendly Australian woman explained to us, that the most crucial part of the application is the medical examination. Australia is very strict and rigid in passing medical examinations making sure that all migrants entering the country were free from any form of disease or illness. Without complications, normally the earliest issue of visa is within the year from application lodgement.

This time I was praying the reverse way… instead of asking God to expedite our application, I was praying for a delay, due to Tatay's serious health condition. But then again, I just left it all to God's will. I let it go and let God!

After six months, we received a letter from the Australian Embassy, stating a weird statement: "The Australian Department of Immigration / Health Department needs an explanation and follow up with your official medical team who examined you last March 1986. Discrepancy on the male applicant showing menstrual period?"

"What! This is totally insane!" were the words of Stephen after reading the shocking letter.

I pacified him and told him to calm down, so we could plan out our next steps.

In the meantime, Tatay's condition had quickly deteriorated and he was just contented in staying at our house, quietly watching tv and secretly asking Matthew or Jasmine to buy him cigarettes.

The doctor told us to give everything he wanted, so I gave up with my usual forbiddance of his smoking and just let him enjoy the short life he had left. We regularly asked him what he wanted to eat and what comfort we could give him. He simply smiled and no words uttered.

His tired and exhausted face and body made him look so weak! So, we just recalled all his favourite food and listed them for the daily planned menu as our quick guide for cooking and so, we can provide him with his favourite things to eat.

Before the Christmas hustle and bustle in the city, very early in the morning, the whole family travelled for the second time to see the official medical team who examined us last March. The children were all excited because they wanted to see the beautiful Christmas decorations in the city, especially the colourful and different kinds of lanterns displayed along the streets. Stephen could not get over the negligence and irresponsible handling of our official documents and even thought of suing the team, for delaying us a year with our application! During the travel to the city, I prayed the rosary with one intention of pacifying Stephen and touch his heart with peace and not to pursue his drastic plan. When we reached the city, I requested that we pass by the church nearby and attend mass, since it was still early for our two o'clock afternoon appointment. I held his hands praying for him and I felt he got the message! Then we had our lunch in one of the nearby-eateries, and basked in the delight of watching the children absolutely enjoying the food.

Still feeling anxious, we arrived at the reception, welcomed by a student nurse who politely guided us inside the hospital director's office. As soon as we entered the room and asked us to sit, the director spoke calmly and humbly expressed his sincere apology for the mix up of documents. He further said that he understood our anger and frustration around this unforgivable negligence and was willing to compensate any damage that it caused. With those sincere words of apology and words of acceptance of their own failure, I think softened and touched Stephen's heart. The Holy Spirit touched his soul to be calm and just be forgiving!

Thank you, Lord God for answering my prayers!

The nurse went inside the medical room and called us for the second time to rectify the discrepancy in the document. The details of my monthly menstruation were wrongly recorded in Stephen's record, which of course shocked the Australian Department of Health, to see a document of a male with a menstruation record! Everything was fixed and successfully ended that saga! Praise God!

We celebrated Christmas to the fullest! After the midnight mass, we invited Kuya Nico and family, Liam to our house and had our 'Noche Buena' our traditional midnight dinner with Pan Americano bread, ham and cheese, traditional slow-cooked Asado and Sopas, Suman and glutinous rice Purple Yam cake. Everyone enjoyed the food, including Tatay, who was unable to taste everything, but he enjoyed the soup and Pan Americano with ham and cheese!

Of course, the children couldn't wait for their gifts, most especially the surprises waiting for them from Santa for being good boys and girls! The whole household cheerfully sang Christmas carols and watched the fireworks from the streets, as celebration for the birth of our Saviour Jesus Christ! We all lovingly hugged, kissed and greeted each other "A Merry and Blessed Christmas!" That was indeed the most beautiful and glorious Christmas celebration and gathering we've ever had!

4. Goodbye Tatay

May 20, 1987

New Year 1987! Our children covered their ears at the sounds of fireworks, gongs and horns, at the same time found excitement in the traditional jumping as high as they could as a prayer of hope to grow taller and a sign of welcoming the New Year!

Tatay still enjoyed the fireworks show on the tv and ate a little bit of the food we prepared for midnight. It was a quiet night for us, because our two nieces Sen and Rosie, went home to their own family; Kuya Nico and family had their midnight dinner at Norma's parents; Jade spent time with her mother, Nanay Julie on festive seasons and school holidays; and my cousin Bella also spent the festive seasons with her mother and siblings in her home town. Only Liam was with us and was busy lighting with the sparklers with the three children, who absolutely enjoyed seeing the colourful bright lights!

People went back to their normal day to day routine. Liam stayed with us fulltime, since Tatay needed some assistance with dressing himself because of his swollen arm due to some cancerous nodes. I could see him becoming weaker every day. We all took turns looking after him, including our two nieces.

One Sunday morning, after church, Uncle Pablo and Aunt Torie visited Tatay and told him that it was time to go home to the ancestral house. Tatay was so happy to see them and gladly agreed to their suggestion. Aunt Torie promised him that she will cook delicious food for him every day, and I saw Tatay's smile of approval. When Tatay agreed to the proposal, I promised to visit him every night, after my night's classes and he happily nodded his approval to that commitment. Before the couple left, they told us that Tatay might not live longer, so we must all be prepared. Whatever happened, he was back at his ancestral home. I was peaceful that Tatay was with Kuya Nico, his wife Norma and two children, who lovingly welcomed him back. I found Norma to being a sensible, responsible and patient daughter-in-law during Tatay's stay with them! All praises to You, Oh God Almighty!

As soon as the lent season started, Stephen suggested to convince Tatay to do the sacraments of reconciliation and extreme unction, which I absolutely concurred. As well, I had contemplated to arrange a meeting with Nanay Julie for reconciliation because since the time they went their separate ways, there was no communication between them. Jade, then a teenager, totally agreed that her parents meet and forgive each other. These hope, intentions and prayers were all answered in God's grace and mercy! Once again, I was so ecstatic to see both Tatay and Nanay Julie at peace with one another.

On the 16th of May 1987, we had celebrated Tatay's 61st birthday with simple thanksgiving gathering with my siblings and Uncle Pablo and family. He was still strong enough to blow his birthday candle. He was so happy that day and even finished the tiny piece of cake which Norma gave him. I noticed that he simply looked at each of us, from his eldest son Kuya Nico and family, then to myself and family, then to Liam and then to his youngest daughter Jade.

Tatay's unusual gestures never missed my keen eyes and made me wonder about that!

Was it only me who noticed that?

After his birthday, he started getting very weak and couldn't stand anymore. Kuya Nico and Norma patiently washed him daily and changed his clothes, with a light spray of refreshing cologne, as suggested by Liam. Four days after his birthday, he had completely deteriorated and his eyes remained almost always closed, so Liam called the doctor to see what was going on. Sadly, the doctor said that he was already in a comatose state and we would only probably just be waiting for the inevitable to happen in a few hours. We all gathered together and started a prayer vigil. I led the rosary, until we had completed two rounds of the three mysteries. I saw his lips moving during prayers, then he slowly opened his eyes looked at me and glanced at Liam. I knew this was his way of telling me to make sure that Liam was settled down before leaving him, as he knew about our migration application.

"Don't worry Tatay, your wish will be granted," I whispered near his ear. Soon after whispering this promise, I saw his last drop of tears from his eyes and heard his last breath.

Then he was gone home to the place, where the Heavenly Father prepared for him. "Eternal rest grant unto Tatay's soul, Oh Lord and let perpetual light shine upon him. May his soul rest in peace. Amen."

The very first night after Tatay's funeral, as usual our family prayed the rosary and then after that, the children immediately went to bed feeling tired after the long and sorrowful day. Poor kids, they must have felt so sad losing their loving grandpa, like we did!

Stephen and I went to the kitchen to have our last cup of tea and reflected on all that had occurred during the year. I told him how I was so anxious about our migration application, and I couldn't envision myself leaving my very sick father. I surrendered everything into God's hands! Then our medical check-up saga delayed our visa because of the documentation error! I told him how I felt so peaceful about that mistake, for I was able to focus completely on Tatay's situation and spent more quality time with him. God ended Tatay's pains and sufferings and took him to his eternal home and reunited with Nanay! I couldn't control my tears of mixed emotions of sorrow and joy, as we lovingly embraced each other! Again, God showed His Almighty Power! Indeed, God works in mysterious ways!

Praise You Lord God!

CHAPTER 7

Farewell to our Beloved Motherland

"Be valiant and strong, do not fear or tremble before them, for the Lord your God is with you; He will not leave you or abandon you."
(Deuteronomy 31:6)

1. Tatay's First Death Anniversary

May 20, 1988

With feelings of guilt, Liam realised how Tatay was never happy with all his wrong doings and the bad reputation he caused the family. He could not forgive himself for what he had done. Stephen consoled him and said, "Tatay was gone physically, but his spirit knows your transformation and very proud of you! Just continue the way you do things at this present time, keep busy with your new job and avoid the wrong crowd and Tatay will rejoice in heaven!" I reassuringly affirmed Stephen's words and he kept those consoling words in his heart. True enough, Liam miraculously and completely turned his life around!

He was doing well with his job and occasionally volunteered to shoulder food for the Sunday's family gathering. Everyone in the family moved on and continued with their daily routine. The children were getting bigger and cheekier.

Again, it was Lenten season which meant that the next month, on the 20th of May, we will celebrate Tatay's first death anniversary! Aunt Torie volunteered to coordinate with the church regarding mass and novena prayers; Kuya Nico and Norma, to organise the cleaning of the burial site in the cemetery; Jade and our two nieces, to look after the flowers for the church and cemetery; while Liam, myself and Stephen, to organise our thanksgiving fellowship with relatives and friends at home with a simple breakfast-lunch menu, commonly known as "brunch".

Everything went smoothly, as planned! We all felt the joy of having the spirit of love, unity and harmony in our family and we knew that Tatay and Nanay rejoiced in heaven and proud of all of us here on earth!

The following month in June, we received an envelope from the Australian embassy! With my trembling fingers, I could hardly open it! I decided to leave it unopened and wait for Stephen, while I continued cooking for dinner, before everyone got home. The children were already doing their homework, and eager to finish everything before eating.

After our meal, Stephen gathered everyone around and showed them an envelope we just received from the Australian embassy. I noticed Liam's uneasiness upon hearing the word embassy. Stephen pulled out the letter and read it aloud! I was so nervous of waiting for a word of either 'rejection or approval.' I hugged and comforted Liam as soon as Stephen finished reading the letter of approval! I told him, "Don't worry, everything will be alright.

Don't you see? God has a plan for all of us. All we do is follow it."

When everyone was in bed, we asked Liam to stay, so we could talk further about his plan.

The whole household knew that the Australian embassy approved our application and issued our migrant visa valid until December 1988. In order words, we had to leave the country before the year ended. Stephen asked Liam to get married before our departure and we will assist him. He immediately replied and said that he was ready to marry Evelyn, a long-time friend and neighbour. "Perfect," Stephen said. The next day they went to meet Evelyn's parents for a formal marriage proposal! We thank you Lord for this big surprise to our family. Thank you for your guidance and putting everything in order. Praise God!

2. Flights vs Financial Woes

The date of flight from Manila to Sydney that we eyed to get was scheduled to fly on October 22, 1988 at eleven o' clock at night, just four days after Liam's wedding on October 18. We asked the travel agent the total amount of money needed to shoulder all five of us.

To my disappointment I said, "Oh, my God, we have a shortfall!" Then Stephen stood up and requested the agent to wait for him for half an hour. I had no idea what was on his mind, but I had prayed fervently for God's miracle! True to Stephen's words, he came back sooner than expected. Then Stephen surprisingly told the agent that the shortfall will be handed to him tomorrow at noon time, and the kind agent considerably agreed.

The next day, all our plane tickets were ready and we all started to sell some of our saleable belongings and pack for our flight the following month! My feelings were indescribable!

These mixed emotions of joy, sorrow and apprehension made my stomach upset, which also resulted in a headache and a slight temperature. Stephen gave me paracetamol and told me to lie down and rest. After our night prayers, Stephen reassured me that there was nothing to worry about the money he borrowed from the money lender with high interest!

(Also referred to as 'loan sharks')

He promised me that as soon as we arrived Australia, he will exert his very best effort and ability to quickly pay the loan. I trusted him and as always, he'd proved himself true to his words. I was so peaceful that night and knowing I could fully concentrate on the upcoming marriage of Liam and Evelyn!

3. Nuptials of Liam and Evelyn

October 18, 1988

On the glorious morning of October 18, 1988, the beautiful bride finally arrived and as soon as she stepped out of the car, the priest signalled the pianist to start the bridal procession towards the front of the altar. I saw Liam's eyes gleam with tears of joy and sorrow. Some of our relatives were present like Uncle Pablo and Aunt Torie, Uncle Esting and some of Liam's close friends. Everyone felt peaceful and perfectly happy for Liam and prayed for a new and blessed life with Evelyn! How we both wished Tatay was around, and I quickly consoled myself that he was present in spirit!

The priest gave his final blessing and asked the people present to welcome the newly married couple with the round of applause! All praises to You, Oh Lord God Almighty!

Our clan and Evelyn's family had the grandiose wedding lunch at our ancestral home. All the young ladies decorated the whole house with white hanging curtains, adorned with colourful and different fragrant flowers, long tables covered with white cloth and chairs catered for around fifty to sixty guests. There were lots of cooked traditional dishes, and of course the celebration wouldn't be complete without the 'whole roasted pig' in the middle of the table! The priest led the prayers and wishes for Liam and Evelyn and blessed the food. I could see that everybody enjoyed the sumptuous lunch. Then Liam stood up and emotionally gave his thanksgiving speech addressed to the guests and mentioned especially Stephen and myself for our absolute love and utmost care for him and said, "They both have never given up on me!"

Everyone started the tinkling sounds of their glasses signalling the newlywed couple to kiss each other and they did! Everybody left late in the afternoon, felt fully blessed in the spirits of love, peace and joy! Indeed, this day and month of October was a memorable and unforgettable day for Liam and Evelyn, as their month of unity in the sacrament of marriage as husband and wife forever!

Right after Liam's wedding, all our saleable belongings were sold. Our very own precious Becky and her thirteen piglets were sold to a good family in the next town with a very impressive price because of her breed. Within three years, Becky had three pregnancies giving us no less than thirteen piglets each time. The sale of Becky and the piglets had contributed a lot in buying our plane tickets!

Early morning of the following day, the buyer arrived at home, to pick up Becky with her thirteen piglets. The whole family shed tears, especially the children who loved her dearly, as they all stroked her huge body and kissed her goodbye. With sadness in our hearts, we all went back inside the house to finalise our luggage and last checks on our documents. After lunch, we cleaned the whole house and made sure it was spotless. I felt nostalgic as I recalled the memories of Tatay's stay in this house. I saw him very comfortable and peaceful with us and loved his special corner spot in the house, as he sat in his favourite chair and watched tv or listened to his favourite music, over a cup of coffee and cigar. I could feel his presence and knew how proud and happy he was for our family's future.

Oh Lord God of All Knowing, thank You for Your mysterious ways!

4. Departure Blessings

October 22, 1988

"This is it! There is no turning back," were Stephen's words as we had a last look at the house upon departing for Manila's international airport. Our family's "despedida", or send off consisted of a big entourage, including Stephen's father, Kuya Nico, Liam, Jade, our two nieces and my cousin Bella, all sat inside the spacious thirteen-seater jeepney including our six luggage, then followed by loud claps of cheers and joy for we all managed to fit inside this vehicle! Recalling that day, the driver was the only one with bulky, stocky stature, the rest of us were all skinny, so there was no issue at all with space!

We were about to leave, when an old woman purposely went to see us in order to extend her best wishes and God's blessings upon us! Looking at her, I was trying to recall who she was and failed to recognise her. Then she said, directly looking at me, "You don't know me at all, but I knew you since your mother passed away. You grew up to be a lovely and talented woman even without a mother. But I misjudged you on your wedding day, for choosing a man like your husband, whom I wrongly judged as well as a nobody! I came to deeply apologise for my misjudgement." She was in tears out of her guilt, so I hugged her and said, "I understand and I forgive you. God bless you." Apologising to me wasn't enough for her, as she hastily walked towards the front of the jeepney to see Stephen and apologised too.

Then finally, she gave us her parting words, "May God be with you always!"

It was so emotional at the airport. Really, I don't like goodbyes! Liam was the most hysterical out of all of them, because he felt like he was losing a mother, which I reciprocated as I too, felt like I was losing a son. Jade was also in tears, as I hugged her tightly. Stephen and I assured all of them that we will regularly write them letters of update.

We kissed and hugged each other after saying a short prayer of protection and thanksgiving.

"It's bye for now, till we meet again. I love you all. You all take care of yourselves and God bless," were my last words to my beloved family. Stephen was also teary eyed as he hugged his father.

Our family followed the queue of the departure's check in area. I was a bit worried when it was our turn to be checked by the migration officer. He was meticulously checking each of our respective documents and I was overwhelmingly relieved, when he said, "Go ahead, all good!" He surprisingly said these uplifting words, "Such a lovely family!" Oh God, he must be God's angel affirming our migration to Australia as His plan for us! Those beautiful and inspiring words had clearly unfolded the reason why Stephen wasn't a successful overseas contract worker, because God wanted us to be together as a family. I controlled the burst of my emotions and just walked straight without turning back, as I looked forward to a better future. Praise God Almighty!

The children were all so excited to board the Qantas Boeing 747 Jumbo Jet, especially Matthew who wanted to be a pilot in the future. It was now boarding time and as we all went inside the spacious, clean and bright plane, I could hear all the giggles of joy from the children, especially the youngest Lily, who's so inquisitive and full of questions! "This is now your future, my dear children, God bless us all," were my words to our lovely children!

It was a fast and quiet night for all of us and surprisingly woke up with the glorious rays of the morning sun peeping through the airplane's window. I opened it and the children were all in awe and wide-eyed to see the white clouds outside the airplane's window! Then the pretty and elegant looking flight attendant served us with a delicious Australian breakfast, as well as coffee and chocolate milk which the children loved and enjoyed!

After an hour, everyone was asked to settle down and put seatbelts on for it was nearly landing time. We were all amazed to see the vastness of Australia as viewed from above, the colourful terracotta tiled roofs of uniformed brick houses and the spring blossoms of the gorgeous lilac jacarandas would remain etched in my memory! What a magnificent beautiful country! Praise God, for your protection and we landed safely!

Chapter 8

New Land of Hope and Mission

"I have taken you from the ends of the earth, and called you from its remotest corners, saying to you, "You are my servant, I have chosen you and have not rejected you." Have no fear, for I am with you; be not dismayed, for I am your God. I will give you strength, and bring you help. I will uphold you with my right hand of justice." (Isaiah 41:9-10)

1. A Migrant Family's Divine Blessings

October 23, 1988

As the whole family exited out of Sydney International Airport's arrival gate, we saw Anthony jubilantly waving at us!

He gave us all warm-welcome hugs and boisterously expressed how happy he was to see us landed safe and sound! Praise God!

Anthony directed us to follow him. Stephen sat with him in the front seat and engaged in vibrant conversation until we had reached their family home, while all of us just looked around in awe of this beautiful and amazing country, so very different from the country we just left!

There was a big colourful WELCOME sign at the front door, then Leni cheerfully came out; hugged every one of us and I had the very last long, tight hug from my loving best friend and sister-in-law! She guided us into their welcoming house with the smell of delicious food emanating from the kitchen and then heard another sweet greeting from their only daughter, gorgeous twelve-year-old Krissy! She eagerly took the hands of her three cousins and embraced them like her sisters and brother and invited them to her room. While Leni was preparing the table, Anthony arranged the freshly cooked food on the table and prepared cold drinks.

He led the prayers of thanksgiving and prayer before meal. The children were not shy at all in joining us in the conversation, as Leni loved asking them questions about the trip. Each of the children eagerly expressed their amazement about the 747 Qantas plane, and added their love for the food served during the flight! Towards the end of our welcome lunch party, Anthony stood up and raised his wine glass and said, "Cheers to the newly arrived migrants and a warm welcome to Australia! And everybody said, "Cheers!" and all the four children cheerfully clapped their hands, while we, the adults drank our wine! All of us really enjoyed the sumptuous Australian lunch that Leni and Anthony had prepared for us! Thank you, Lord God for the kindness and hospitality of this lovely family!

Leni showed us our rooms and suggested that we freshened up and made sure we feel at home! Krissy again invited the children to her room to play the whole afternoon and they didn't come out until dinner time.

Leni and I had plenty of time catching up with our stories of struggles and success regarding our application! She was in tears when I had shared with her the story about Tatay. She was so thankful and felt blessed that she had the chance to talk to him at our house and wished him to get well soon, so he could come to Australia as well!

Monday morning, as Leni planned the previous night, we went to the Department of Social Security (now called Centrelink) to register as newly arrived migrants in order to get some welfare benefits. Right after that, Leni guided us to the nearest state school, to enrol the children, which was fortunately, only a stone's throw away from their house, without even crossing the road! We went home for late lunch and left the children with Leni and Krissy, while Stephen and I took the train towards the city to personally apply at the famous company, Hoover, which just advertised hiring workers after three months of closure due to union issues. We were blessed to get this information, while we were at the Department of Social Security. A young Filipino looking man seated at the corner overheard that we were newly arrived migrants and he eagerly introduced himself as Ralph. He happily shared with us that he just personally filed his application at Hoover as a process worker and that they were currently still hiring workers. To me, Ralph was God's messenger to inform us this good news, and guide our way to our next step!

Stephen looked at the time, which was just one o'clock in the afternoon and decided to go for a train trip into the city after we enrolled the children into the local state school.

At Hoover, the friendly receptionist called our names and instructed us to complete the application forms. When she checked the completed forms, she looked so surprised to know that we just arrived yesterday. "Why are you in a hurry to work? Maybe spend your time to see this new country first?" she politely asked with a gentle smile. Stephen was quick to reply and boldly said, "Oh yes, that would be nice to do, but we are in a hurry to earn money to pay off our loan. But of course, we will certainly spend time to see around this beautiful country!" The friendly receptionist just simply nodded and smiled at Stephen. She continued looking through the required documents and then finally said, "Since you just arrived yesterday, you both don't need any medical examinations from us and you can start next Monday at seven o'clock in the morning! Congratulations!"

Thank you, Lord, for all these countless blessings! What a productive and blessed Monday!

All of us enjoyed our train trips and sight-seeing around Sydney, the glorious Sydney Harbour's sunrise, the unique architectural beauty of the Sydney Opera house, the perfect structural design of the famous Sydney Harbour Bridge and the endless rides at Luna Park!

Then the following day, Leni guided us to Bicentennial Park at Sydney Olympic Park, which was just fully established that year 1988, to protect and conserve Homebush Bay's remaining wetlands. It was named Bicentennial to celebrate 200 years of Australia being a country. Indeed, the children were all overwhelmed with what they had experienced during the first week in Australia! Thanks to our kind and generous tourist guide Leni!

The children eagerly started their schooling and excited to meet new friends in the school, as well as in the neighbourhood. They seemed to be settling very fast in their new environment!

That very first weekend from our arrival, Anthony impressed us with his expertise of lamb and steak barbeque, grilled sausages and corn with freshly baked bread and garden salad!

"So, a typical Australian menu," Leni said. We had a sumptuous and delicious lunch in their big backyard with native trees and a huge jacaranda tree which was still in full bloom, the lilac flowers falling down and beautifying the ground like a magical carpet in a fairy land!

At night, after the family dinner, all the children prepared their school bags and uniforms for next day's school, while I prepared their snacks and lunches. Then Leni put the kettle on for tea and called us before retiring to bed. She was impressed and overjoyed with the smooth sailing of our first week: the registration at the Department of Social Security, enrolment of the kids to school, the enjoyable tour in the city and most of all our super-fast employment blessing!

Stephen politely told Leni that as soon as we received our first weekly pay, we will share financial support for our stay at their house, while looking for our own place. Leni totally disagreed to the idea, in fact she said, that Anthony and her decided not to accept any monetary payment from us, but rather wanted us to save up for our own place and added that we can stay as long as we wanted to! Both Stephen and I were surprised at their acts of utmost generosity and kindness of heart! Stephen quickly stood up and lovingly embraced her sister and brother-in-law! We all fondly hugged each other and said our good nights! Praise God!

2. Stephen's Health Scare

From Leni's house, it was a ten-minute-walk to the train station. It took us almost one hour to reach our destination and ended with another ten-minute walk to Hoover.

What a huge manufacturing plant! As we entered the main gate, the security guard signalled us to show him our ids and gave us instructions where to go and whom to see. I was a bit nervous and apprehensive, because this has never been my line of work! Without hesitation, I willingly went along with Stephen in applying as a process worker because my priority was to gain stability financially for our family's sake. Everyday our loan was earning interest and we aimed to pay it off as soon as we can. To land into any fast money earning job was my main goal upon arrival. I swallowed my pride and just simply forgot my career as I left our country and landed in a new horizon to begin a better one for the children's brighter future!

The personnel clerk introduced me to the supervisor of the 'Hoovermatic' production line, whom I found a dignified and respectable person at first impression. This was the production line I was assigned, which was a line of one of the models of Hoover's small washing machines, with a built-in function of a dryer. This was the famous and best-selling washer at that time due to its dual function. Stephen was assigned in the other building, where the majority were men due to the nature of their assembly line, which were mainly the major components like drums, shafts, transmissions, and other big parts of washers and dryers. This American owned assembly plant, established in 1954 manufactures washing machines, clothes dryers, refrigerators and vacuum cleaners, with approximately one thousand assemblers at that main plant. I felt so blessed to be a part of the production line where I was assigned due to its lightness and simplicity of operation meant for women.

Thank You, Lord!

As one whole family, we felt the Hands of God guiding us in the right direction. The children had quickly settled in their new school, based on their story telling during dinner time and their home works and impressive test results. At the same time, Stephen and I enjoyed our own respective jobs, especially on Thursdays when the payroll officer personally handed us our weekly pay! We agreed to shop for food and groceries weekly and also cooked for the whole family household in order to replace the kindness and generosity of Leni and Anthony.

I saw in Leni's eyes joy and contentment, every day as she arrived from work and smelt the delicious food coming from the kitchen. She really appreciated our voluntary offering in cooking our everyday meals, which I thought was just fair to repay them for letting us stay, rent-free, with them. She was just so delighted and felt excited every time she went home, curious to know what dish we cooked for dinner! Such a simple way to make one immensely happy!

It was nearly the end of November, when Stephen woke up uncomfortable, complaining of pain on his left leg. I took a look at it and noticed his swollen knee! We decided to miss work and went to see the local doctor, whose clinic was just a few houses away, which was perfect as Stephen struggled to walk. After checking his leg and knee, he gave us the telephone number of a rheumatologist to call and make appointment. That night, we prayed the rosary for the special intention of Stephen's healing. All the children were so quiet and sad to see their dad in pain. When the lights were off, I went to the bathroom just to be alone and burst out my worries to the Lord, as I cried out to Him, "Lord God, I know You will bring help and give me strength!" I stayed there for almost an hour just feeling God's presence in silence. He is All Knowing, so I totally surrendered my anxiety and worries about Stephen's health condition. We were just barely a month in this country, blessed with instant jobs, but now facing this big challenge! I offered everything to His Holy Name and let go, then went to bed with comfort and peace in my heart!

We missed one week's work due to all the medical check-ups. At night, I felt so tired and exhausted because I was doing chores solely, normally shared with Stephen. I insisted that he just laid down or sit with his feet up. On Monday, he was scheduled to have the procedure called a joint aspiration, wherein fluid will be removed from the knee joint using a needle and syringe, done under a local anaesthetic to relieve swelling and obtain fluid for analysis. It was successfully done. Praise God! The specialist gave him medications and medical certificate to be submitted at work and gave him another week to rest. I already worked the following day, so that I could hand in Stephen's medical certificate. While I was traveling alone, I was praising and thanking God that we didn't spend a single cent on medical bills! Everything was free, including the procedure! Another big surprise was that our weekly pay slips were complete. The payroll officer replied when I asked the question, "I was confident that you will submit the medical certificates very soon." Thank you, Oh Lord!

Stephen was allowed to go back to work, but with double crutches to support the painful leg. At work, his supervisor gave him light duties like recording the daily production report of four assembly lines next to each other and monitoring the number of specific parts needed in some production lines. It was like a clerical job with less walking. How kind and considerate was his boss and every one within the company! I was absolutely relieved with everything that had occurred in the past three weeks and felt confident that Stephen was heading towards a full recovery! Praise God for Your Healing Power, Love and Protection!

Every December, the factory shuts down for maintenance work and so all workers were forced to take their annual leave, with the exceptions of few workers who volunteered to stay during the shut-down. Unexpectedly, Stephen's boss asked him if he wanted to work through, which he gladly and thankfully accepted. His supervisor still gave him light duties to my surprise! I stayed with the children who were on school holidays and was able to do lots of cleaning and gardening aside from the everyday household chores. Our children helped too with the chores like cleaning their rooms, hanging clothes and washing the dishes.

They knew and remembered very well the words from their dad, "Our family is a team and be the best team player." So, at a very young age, they'd already helped in their own little ways, like fixing their own beds or as simple as wiping the table or sorting the freshly washed clothes. Leni was actually dazzled how disciplined the kids were and knew exactly what they had to do in their everyday activities. They were trained to maintain the sink in a spotless and shiny condition by washing any kitchen utensil like glasses, or plates they'd used and put them away clean and dry. I kept telling them that they're like angels helping Mom and certainly, made Mom very happy, with their obedience and impressive behaviour, I made sure, that after work, I brought something they would surely love like chocolates, lollies or blue berry muffins. My whole day's tiredness and fatigue would all vanish, once I saw their wide eyes gleaming with extreme joy, combined with their endless giggles, upon opening the "magic bag" containing the goodies! Indeed, simple things are the best things in life!

Leni and Anthony still worked as normal and very appreciative of having delicious home-cooked meals everyday ready for our family dinner. And for the very first time with this school break, they weren't worried about Krissy, because of my presence and the children.

Leni kept saying, "What will I do without you?!"

3. Our Priceless Castle

Three months later, I woke up very early in the morning, as if I was still dreaming! I was in tears in front of our altar praying and thanking the Lord for blessing us our own little humble dwelling, our very own priceless castle!

Before Christmas, Noel, a real estate agent went to see us about a property available for sale. The owner desperately wanted her property to be sold as quickly as possible to look after her sick mother, who lived in another state. We were blessed to have saved enough money for a house deposit and this gave us the confidence to make a commitment to the offer. Noel made an appointment with the owner, who was also a migrant like us and gladly offered us a good deal. Stephen and I, after inspections, absolutely loved the house and decided to accept the deal. Without needing to wait for settlement, much to our surprise, the owner allowed us to move into the house just in time for the start of the school term in February 1989.

Indeed, it was unbelievable how we were able to acquire our very own house in such a short period of time! Truly, with God nothing is impossible! As the scripture says in Matthew 19:26, "For human beings this is impossible, but for God all things are possible."

Leni was shocked, but genuinely happy for our astonishing achievement! When she asked me the question, "How on earth did you manage to buy a house within three months of arrival!"

I simply replied, "There were so many angels sent by God and you are one of them. With God and your kindness of heart and generosity, it paved the way for this fruition."

In a small utility vehicle with a trailer, we fitted all our luggage, which wasn't a lot, and a double bed given by Leni and we were all set for another exodus!

I don't like goodbyes! With tears in my eyes, I kissed and hugged Leni and she knew what I felt without saying a single word. She was also very sad, but really happy and proud of us!

This was it! We were set to the destined place where God directed us!

The children were all excited to play in the spacious backyard, in a secured battle axe location, which was the main reason why we bought this property, for the children's protection and safety. A battle axe block is a block of land situated behind another, with access to the street through a narrow driveway. Its shape is like a battle axe, wherein the narrow driveway is the handle and the main property where the house is situated is the head. It was the perfect location for the children's freedom to play inside the gated property with no fear of any danger from moving vehicles on the street. It was a carpeted, brick veneer, three-bedroom house with a small porch at the front entry and a balcony at the back. It was elevated with six steps entering through the front, with aligned ferns and colourful birds of paradise along all the sides of the house. As we unpacked the six boxes, we only had, which we brought from the Philippines, the children took their own clothes and instantaneously arranged them in the rooms we assigned to them accordingly.

Enthusiastically, they fixed and beautified their own rooms. Matthew, being the only boy, had one room to himself with the double bed given by his Aunt Leni. Jasmine and Lily shared the other room, with a wooden bunk bed, generously given to us by the previous owner. Stephen and I, of course occupied the master's bedroom, which we hadn't touched yet. We prioritised to set up and arrange our family altar, so the pictures of Mother Mary and Jesus, which we brought with us could be properly hanged, with the lights to be connected too, ready for tonight's very first family Rosary in our new beloved humble abode. We moved into our priceless castle, without a washing machine, refrigerator, television, not even a radio! Jasmine and Lily patiently helped me washed our clothes by hand using the bathtub. After a month, we were so delighted to see Stephen unloading a second-hand washing machine, which he bought from the appliances shop nearby! A newly found friend in the suburb gave us a twelve-inch black and white tv, which entertained children during their rest time, when they got tired from playing cricket out in the backyard. The most essential appliance was still missing! We desperately needed a refrigerator to preserve food from spoilage, especially milk and other dairy products. So, Stephen asked his other sister if she had a spare refrigerator and luckily, she had one!

Jubilantly, we were all set in our new dwelling, our own priceless castle! Praise God!

The children again quickly settled in their new school, environment and met new friends from their school, as well as the neighbourhood. We were able to move around and discover the local shops, doctor and church. Due to the short distance of our house to the school, the children were not given bus passes, so they had no choice but to walk to school.

They didn't mind at all, because of the presence of the new friends they'd met who they cheerfully walked to school together with, like long-time friends!

Stephen and I couldn't believe that we were living independently after barely three months of arriving in this new land of hope! This humble dwelling is our priceless castle given to us by God, as a roof over our heads, shelter from the soaring heat of the sun, strong wind, heavy rain and furious storms, and mainly the little shrine of our family, with God in the midst of us! Thank You, Oh Lord God Almighty!

4. Unified Family as a Working Team

"*L*ord God of Mercy, show and guide us the way in paying off our loan in the Philippines."

This prayer of petition was always included in our daily family prayer. It had been six months since we borrowed the money and would have earned a lot of interest! Our weekly wages were just enough to pay our mortgage, food and amenities. Though we wanted to enrol the children in private Catholic schools, we couldn't afford the expensive school fees for three children. We had no choice but to enrol them all in public schools with only minimal fees to pay, as public schools receive government subsidy for all other related costs. The children knew our financial standing, as well as the loan we had left back in our motherland. All of them were supportive of our decisions and were willing to help in any little way they could.

They understood clearly the importance of unity and team work in a family.

One Friday afternoon, an educational insurance agent knocked at our door and said that he brought us some brochures for our children's college educational plans. Stephen gladly let him in and offered him cold drinks, as he noticed him sweating due to the hot weather.

Gratefully, he introduced himself as Nick and started asking us questions until he offered us what he was selling. I told him honestly about our financial situation, which he sensibly understood. He kept all the documents in his briefcase and gave us his calling card for future reference. He was about to go, when all of a sudden, he asked Stephen if he wanted a part time job. Of course, his answer was a big YES! He gave us another calling card with details of his friend Dom, who owned a plastering business in the city and timely was looking for casual workers! Another angel was sent by God through Nick!

That weekend, Stephen was able to get an early appointment to meet up with Dom. I went with him, as he requested and after an hour's drive to the city, we stopped in front of an old house, with big shed. There we met Dom, an old looking Filipino man, who warmly welcomed us inside and offered us cold drinks. Then he eagerly showed us all these different kinds of figurine moulds, which he creatively made, ready to be filled up with plaster. That's why he needed workers to be trained on the process. Stephen gladly accepted the challenge and Dom started training him right there and then!

After six hours, Dom was happy and satisfied with the finished products processed by Stephen and trustingly told him to bring forty different moulds of his choice and start making them at home after his work or even on weekends. All the finished products must be polished and he will pick them up fortnightly with the corresponding cash payment. That was an amazing huge surprise for both Stephen and I! Straight away, we both thought of our loan!

Oh! my Lord God Almighty, thank you for answering our prayers! Thank You for sending another angel!

When we reached home, the children were all curious about all those figurine moulds, which their father laid down on the floor. They expressed enthusiasm in helping with this extra job which will be contributing to the quick payment of the loan.

We're so blessed to have such sensible and responsible children! Stephen showed the children the process, but assigned them the easy part which was the polishing part of the finished products.

Matthew, our only son, showed interest in the mixing process, which helped Stephen a lot.

He made him as his right hand. All of us girls, did the cleaning and polishing part! Through firm determination, unity and team work within the family, in two years and a half, we were able to pay off our loan! We praised and acknowledged our children's utmost cooperation and sacrifice as a tremendous part in accomplishing this arduous goal of loan clearance.

They greatly helped and supported us in every little way they could. Indeed, they played a huge part in our success being migrants, empty handed and penniless, with nothing in the beginning. They learned the value of each cent earned and made sure that it was spent wisely.

I remembered clearly how our children were deprived of the newly manufactured toys and gadgets like Nintendo, X-box, etc during those times, and never we heard them complain for they knew very well that these were not essentials. They were trained to prioritise their needs, not their wants. As early as October, we explored Kmart and told them to select whatever they want to have as Christmas present and we paid it through "lay-by" and made sure we collected them on or before the first week of December in time to wrap and place them under the Christmas tree! During the opening of gifts, Stephen and I managed to give them extra gifts which we'd thought would surprise them. Wide-eyed with gleams of joy and shouts of gladness could be heard with the tune of Christmas carols, as we lovingly greeted, hugged and kissed each other endlessly, while we thanked and praised the birth of baby Jesus, our Saviour and Redeemer! Happy Birthday Baby Jesus!

With our family's presence of love, perseverance, harmony and teamwork and most importantly through God's blessings and guidance, we were able to overcome that biggest hurdle in our lives. Thank You, Oh Lord God for blessing us three angels from heaven, our very own loving and caring children! Praise be to God!

5. Family Mission

Since Dom's figurine moulds were returned, our family gained freedom from having the extra work on weekends. We found the children so extremely happy and eagerly moved on to their normal lives as active teenagers. They cheerfully looked forward to the weekends to join their friends' trip into the city and watched football games. Stephen and I were so thankful and over joyous to see them in their different activities just like typical adolescents. They certainly deserved enjoyment and leisure which they missed in the last two years and a half because of the family's extra work on weekends.

46 Years After ... "The Sign"

One Sunday morning, Stephen received a call from a lovely couple Lucas and Naomi from our church and asked if it's okay to drop by for a quick visit. He joyfully said yes to it and in fact, looked forward to see them!

Lucas and Naomi had been faithfully inviting us to join this Catholic community called Couples for Christ, since the time we had settled in that area. Unfortunately, we did not respond to it, due to our work commitment with Dom on weekends. Just in the nick of time, God once again showed us His great love and answered our prayers by sending this lovely couple along the way to evangelise us into this charismatic organisation, meant for family renewals and spiritual enrichment, in which we were so interested to know more of.

This time, we willingly responded to this invitation. Lucas and Naomi personally visited us at home and explained what the community is all about. We were so happy to know that its mission is for 'Families in the Holy Spirit Renewing the Face of the Earth,' which was actually the kind of community we were looking for! Then enthusiastically they broke the great news that there will also be a youth group to be launched very soon, which fired us up more, because we wanted the children to be with a youth group with the same faith! We clearly remembered our mentors saying, "Tell me who your friends are and I will tell you who you are." This is affirmed in the passage from Psalm 13:20 saying, "He who walks with wise men grows wise, but with fools suffers harm!" So, as parents, we recognised the value and importance of the kind of peer group our children should have and environment that they are surrounded with.

So, in 1991, Stephen and I officially became members of Couples for Christ and the children, as members of Youth for Christ, eventually. We always looked forward to weekends for the Saturday community prayer meetings and then Sunday mass, as well as our own family day.

This was definitely the meaning of my dream in March 1986 about the intertwined hearts, which occurred the night after our application for migration to Australia was lodged. In this dream God conveyed the message of mission upon reaching our destination. This charismatic community that we found, served as an instrument in continuing this mission of evangelisation which we left back home. The children as well became so active in the youth group, until they stepped up as leaders later on.

One time, the leader of the community had commissioned all of us, as a family to travel to Canberra to introduce Youth for Christ. It was indeed a great honour and joy of having our family together in faith and mission! As soon as we entered the house of Bro. Paul, the leader of the group, Lily, our youngest daughter immediately reacted on the picture of two hearts she saw hanging on the wall and said, "Oh Mum, look, your dream!" She was only in pre-school at that time when I told her about my dream. When she arrived home from school, she cheerfully showed me her drawing of the two intertwined hearts. That's why she remembered this dream very well! I was in tears and had goosebumps all over my body for I felt and smelt the presence of God, affirming that we were going in the right direction to following His will and plan for us! After two months, the Canberra brothers and sisters started their Youth program! We Praise and Thank You Lord!

Chapter 9

Fruits of Faith, Love and Sacrifice

"After this, I will pour out my spirit upon all flesh. Your sons and daughters will prophesy, old men will dream dreams, your young men will see visions." (Joel 3:1)

1. Love Until It Hurts

1989-2010

I'd learned to love my job at Hoover! God truly manifested His love and faithfulness, by sending angels again through my assembly line supervisor and my co-workers! At the very start of my work, I was anxious about my capability in performing this kind of work and at the same time worried about the people, I will be working with. But God spoke to me through this Bible verse that very early morning before the start of my first day of work, and the quote says, "Be valiant and strong, do not fear or tremble before them, for the Lord, your God, is with you; he will not leave you or abandon you." (Deuteronomy 31:6)

I felt so at ease and comfortable the moment I met the middle-eastern looking supervisor in his late 60's and gently explained the very specific, but repetitive job I had to do the whole day! To my surprise, I found it easy, which boosted my self-confidence. Then he introduced me to the workers on that line, who were mostly older women coming from different countries in the world. Their welcoming and friendly gestures towards me made me feel at peace, serene and I instantly loved them with that nice feeling of relief, of finding a family!

Thank You, Oh Lord!

That night, Stephen and I exchanged stories about our first day at work, while our children were busy doing their home works. He was impressed with the heavy machineries which were shown to him by his supervisor and scheduled him to be trained almost straight away.

Both of us, just like our children learned quickly to adapt to our environment, at work and at school. But God knew that deep inside me, I wasn't satisfied with my job, because I desperately missed my beloved profession. Two months from our arrival, Leni also helped me to lodge my credentials at the Department of Education to teach high school. While waiting for the results, patiently I worked at Hoover with Stephen and I started to love the environment, especially being with the older women around me, where I learned a lot, from their wisdom and experiences in life as migrants from different cultures. Again, I offered everything to God and ready to accept His will.

After six months, I received a letter from the Department of Education stating that the Department had approved my application as a high school teacher and can immediately start that coming term on 3 July 1989. Of course, I was over the moon and couldn't thank enough God's love and goodness for my answered prayers! Thank You, Oh Lord God Almighty!

I already mentioned this quotation from William Shakespeare before, but let me state it again, "Parting is such a sweet sorrow." I felt joy and at the same time sadness when I received the letter! Yes, I felt the delight and pleasure to be able to practice once again my beloved profession for thirteen years in the Philippines! It did definitely lift up by self-esteem being recognised as a teacher in this first world country! But I had also learned to love my job at Hoover and enjoyed the convenience of going home and completely forgetting about work, as opposed to being a teacher, with endless school plans and work still to be done at home. I had developed a close relationship with my co-workers, especially the older women who supported me in my struggles emotionally. I saw in them the image of my mother, whom I had missed so much, especially being a new migrant. It saddened me again to think of separating from them after I had experienced the love and care they had shown towards me. It was at this point where I had to weigh the pros and cons if I should go ahead and go to my beloved profession or stay in my current job. Again, I was caught at a crossroads! Help me Lord, and show me the right way!

As a new teacher in Australia, I had to study the NSW curriculum and syllabus, as well as read the books required in the certain year I will be assigned. Would time still allow me to help my children with their homework and contribute to our family's extra job? Whereas if I stayed in my current job, upon arriving home, I had the time to prepare our dinner, then concentrate on helping the children with their school assignments, at the same time also have the chance to polish some figurines from the day before. I considered all the advantages and disadvantages of the situation and most of all fervently prayed for discernment and the guidance of the Holy Spirit!

After our night prayers, I asked Stephen's opinion regarding my dilemma. As always, being a man of few words, he simply said, "After praying to the Holy Spirit for enlightenment, follow what your heart says, not your mind."

At 4:30 of Saturday morning, the sound of the alarm clock woke up the whole household, which I forgot to switch off last night because of that hard situation I was in. I quickly turned it off, so the children could go back to sleep and I was happy again to feel the total serenity and quietness in the house and soon heard snoring from the children's rooms. Deep inside me, as I quietly prayed the morning offerings, I felt at peace with my tough decision, which I firmly believed was guided by the

Holy Spirit, because of the presence of total peace and utmost joy in my heart. Giving up my beloved profession for the good of my family led me to contemplate on the glory of Jesus Christ's agony and death on the cross because of His unconditional love for His people. I immensely love my family because, family is everything to me and I could give up anything for its sake, even it hurts. This reminded me of the quotation from Saint Marie Eugene of Jesus, the foundress of the Religious of the Assumption which states, "Sacrifice gives us a complete joy and unites us with God on His infinite Blessedness." God allowed me to taste the noble privilege of recognition in this country as a teacher, but lovingly tested me where truly my heart was!

I faithfully stayed at Hoover, until opportunities came up from internal job openings like clerical and supervisory roles. My supervisor kept informing me when open opportunities eventuate and advised me not to miss any one of them. I was so thankful with his concern and followed his guidance. True enough, with diligence and perseverance, eventually I climbed up the ladder and until I had reached my full satisfaction and contentment. I was determined to remain with the company, which turned out to be like a family to me until my retirement!

Praise God, for leading me the right way! As I quote from Proverbs 3:5-6

> *"Trust in the Lord with all your heart;*
> *do not rely on your own insight. Let*
> *His presence pervade all your ways, and*
> *He will make your paths smooth. "*

2. Growing Pains: Trials and Triumph

*T*ime quickly passed and by 1991, Jasmine turned 14, Matthew 13 and Lily 11. We now had teenagers! This stage of life is commonly called 'the awkward age' because a teenager is too young to be called an adult and too old to be addressed as a child. This is the dangerous period too, as they go through stormy phases emotionally, socially and mentally.

Our biggest concern as parents was the safety of our children particularly around the kind of group they would join, and the type of environment they might end up with.

When we joined Couples for Christ in 1991, God answered our prayers for the great news that very soon, the Ministry of Youth for Christ will be launched, a spiritual group for teens aged 11 to 19 years old. We were over the moon as parents, for we believed that this was the right avenue and perfect place for our teenagers to dwell in; to chill and hang out.

Being full time working parents, we used to leave as early as five o'clock in the morning and arrive home at five o'clock in the afternoon. So, that meant within twelve hours of the day, our children were out of our sight. This made us worry every day and wanted to know where the children would be after school hours and what were they doing. During those times, we didn't have the luxury of mobile phones nor have the 'find my friend' tool. Truly, it was a big challenge for parents to track down where their children were. It was a matter of trusting the children for their sensible decisions and discernment whether to do the right thing or the other way, coupled with endless prayers for God's guidance and protection over them! The daily newspaper commonly printed reports about teenagers becoming drug addicts as young as thirteen years old; young boys and girls caught in robbery; or even horribly found dead because of an overdose. These were just some of the threats and danger out there for us to be overly anxious about with our children's safety.

Indeed, Youth for Christ Ministry was God's answer to our prayers. It played a significant part of our children's strong and steadfast faith and trust in the Lord.

Stephen and I stepped up as a household leader of a group of five lovely couples about fifteen to twenty years older than us. We were indeed honoured and blessed to be with them in our weekly prayer meetings. Through their vast experiences and immense wisdom as parents, we learned a lot particularly in raising and dealing with teenage children.

They affirmed that this was generally the period when family conflicts arise on certain issues like discipline, parent's directions or even unpleasant treatment towards the children, sexuality, dating, friends and school performances. These issues may lead to serious parent-children relationship dissension, if not resolved accordingly. These group of senior-couples, tremendously contributed to the easing and solving our concerns regarding our teenagers. One of the Nanay's told us that during teenage years of children, parents should stop being a domineering parent, but rather be like a best friend and a confidant to the children. She said, "From birth to 12 years of age, our children are totally ours. Once they'd reached 13 years of age, slowly and slowly, they started to loosen their grip on our hands."

Parents must create an open and approachable relationship, so they are not scared to tell you everything. Stop the repetitive words like: "Don't do this and don't do that," otherwise, you declared yourselves as their enemies. Befriend them and spend more time with them in places where teenagers usually hang around like sports complex, cinemas or arcades. Chill out together and be cool parents! I totally agreed with Nanay, but hard on Stephen because of his very disciplined, military-like upbringing. It wasn't easy, but we had to do it, just to develop bonding and harmonious relationship with our children.

Parents-Children Enrichment Retreat was one of the programs of Youth for Christ, which I considered as a gift from heaven, for this helped a lot with reconciliation of family conflicts.

Our own family benefited amazingly from this program. Yes, we had also encountered disputes and disagreement with our children, but we invested time and effort to reach a peaceful and harmonious relationship. First and foremost, we sat down together in prayers and then they took turns opening up about their resentments and with God's grace find the right resolutions. This strategy is called "One on One" with the parents. We experienced challenges and trials in the growing pains of our teenagers, but with constant prayers, openness and respect towards one another, we achieved the most coveted price of victory and triumph! We passed the test with flying colours and received our trophies of success having a loving, caring and unified family!

We exalt and praise Your holy name, Oh Lord God Almighty!

> *"How good and delightful it is to live together in harmony as family." (Psalm 133:1)*

> *"Teach a child the way he should go, and he will not stray from it even when he is old." (Proverbs 22: 6)*

> *"The crown of the aged is their children's children; the children's glory is their parents." (Proverbs 17: 6)*

3. Peace and Contentment in the Family

"If God is with us, who shall be against us" (Romans 8:31) These were the words, I kept repeating to our children as they grew up, which I could see personally, what the effect of this mantra had in their own familial journeys.

"God looks at the simplest things accomplished by man, but done out of great love" were Stephen's favourite words, which he also regularly quoted to the children. In addition to that quotation from their father, I kept reminding them of my favourite quotation, which I had learned from my Uncle Sinto, Tatay's oldest brother, when I was a teenager. He said, "Always keep this in your mind: life is what you make it." I explained this to our children: "It's all your own choices in life, and own decision which path to follow, that would determine the kind of life you would live." This is where the importance of a deep relationship with God comes in, for constant prayers and guidance towards the right course.

As Christian parents, we brought up our children since their formative and developmental years inculcating in them the importance of God's presence in their lives. We faithfully respected Sundays as a day for and with God and our family. These values were enhanced through Couples for Christ community which we gladly joined in 1991 because of its mission statement: "Families in the Holy Spirit, renewing the face of the earth." This was exactly what the Lord conveyed to me in that dream of two intertwined hearts!

As a Christian couple, we can't thank enough God's love and faithfulness to us in leading and guiding us all the way, especially in rearing up our children to be good and responsible son and daughters. Their individual experiences as leaders in the youth group had evolved them to be the kind of persons they are now, which made Stephen and I as the happiest and proudest parents ever! There were of course, some trials and challenges which they encountered during their teenage years, but through persistent prayers and strong faith in God's protection, the Spirit of Goodness, as always had been proven victorious!

Our three children had finished their own respective fields of profession. Jasmine is a manager in a prestigious bank; Matthew, a program manager of a website company, and Lily, an executive assistant in a corporate travel agency. We couldn't be any happier and prouder than what our children had successfully achieved!

In 1998 Jasmine got married to Jeremiah and was blessed with two children, Jean and Jermaine. After five years, in 2003 Matthew married lovely Raelyn and blessed with two children, Raphael and Mae. Another five years later, in 2008 Lily got married to Marty and blessed with two children as well, Christopher and Maya. They are all independently and happily living in their own humble castles!

Analysing the intervals of our children's marriages, there was a gap of five years in each of their marriages. Then, God blessed them all with two children each with a boy and a girl.

Stephen and I'd realised that God, even in our children's marriages, lovingly and faithfully guided them in the right choice of spouse and settled down in the sacrament of Holy Matrimony in an amazing orderly manner!

Indeed, God is a God of order! With the fruits of love from our children's marriages made us now proud grandparents of three handsome boys and three gorgeous girls! Praise God Almighty!

4. Holidays in the Hospital

From the early months of 2003, I could feel this severe pain in my right hip which caused me so much struggle to stand, much alone, walk. Until such time I could not bear the pain anymore, I went to see my local doctor, who immediately gave me a referral to an orthopaedic specialist. The specialist, after analysing my x-ray said that there was no other solution in my hip condition, but a total right hip replacement surgery. I honestly told him that I didn't have a private health fund, so, I would have to be enlisted in the public health system with an eight to twelve month waiting period. The children, out of their love and concern on my severe pain, generously offered to shoulder the private health fund, but with twelve months waiting before I can avail the services. So basically, it had the same waiting time with the public health system. I told everyone that I could wait and just use a walking stick when I walked, to alleviate the pain. In Nov 2003, I enlisted myself for a total right hip replacement, with the hope for an earlier call instead of waiting nearly a year to be called in for surgery.

In April 2004, the children organised a simple celebration for my 50th birthday. I wanted it to be a meaningful and memorable thanksgiving. So, I thought of helping out the poor and the needy. I requested the guests not to give me material gifts, but rather voluntarily give monetary donations which will support a homeless single mother to have her own house built in the Philippines. It was indeed a successful event! To my great surprise, the total donated funds were more than enough to finish the noble project. I sincerely acknowledged every guest for their generosity in participating in the charitable cause! Upon submission of the donated funds to the housing project organisation, I asked for the name and address of the recipient, so I could visit the site. In the report, I firmly requested them to withhold my name and just write from an 'anonymous donor.'

To all the guests who attended my simple celebration I gave them bookmarks with these words of inspiration: "Life is a gift from God; what we do with it, is our gift to God!"

Praise God for experiencing this joy of giving!

46 Years After ... "The Sign"

In June 2004, I just arrived at work, when my phone rang and brought me the good news that I was next in line for surgery, due to some cancellations! I was so ecstatic and I immediately informed my manager, who had shown his full support and concern towards my health condition. He gladly signed my leave for three months and wished me all the best and success with my operation.

My family were all around my bed when I woke up from my major surgery at eight o'clock at night! Looking at them one by one, I could see all their eyes sparkling with tears of joy and relief because I woke up from a long seven hours surgery-sleep, as I glanced briefly at the clock on the wall! I remembered that it was one o'clock in the afternoon when the attendants took me to the operating theatre. No wonder that my loving family had these tears of jubilation and peace when I awoke! Oh Lord, thank you for this successful operation!

In the early morning the following day, my specialist said that my blood pressure was quite low, as well as my potassium levels and I might need to undergo a blood transfusion. When Stephen heard that, he hastily went to buy bananas in order to get my potassium up. After three hours, the nurse checked my blood pressure and potassium and everything was back to normal!

The specialist informed me that I will be staying at the hospital for approximately nine days before they released me and from there, I will be rehabilitated in one of the nearby homes for another three months depending on my recovery progress.

A lot of miracles happened while I was in the hospital. I saw the vision of Mother Mary's silhouette covered with a cape on a switched off tv, with my eldest daughter Jasmine, who also saw that vision! Then I was so privileged to be assigned a solo-patient room with an ensuite bathroom, in which everyone thought I was a private health fund holder. When asked about it, I just agreed to what everyone had assumed! A female patient next to my room, one morning warmly greeted me while on her morning walk and peeped in my room, and was impressed at the comfort I had being on my own, as well as expressed some gestures of jealousy. I was so glad that she just remained quiet and didn't ask any question.

Deep inside me I greatly appreciated this God's blessing for providing me this luxury and comfort of having this HPHF which stands for "Heaven's Private Health Fund."

I considered my nine days in the hospital as the best days of my life! You may ask why?

First of all, I knew that I was not alone in my room for I was being watched over by God and Mother Mary like a child wrapped in their loving arms filled with love and utmost care!

Secondly, it was a miracle that I was assigned in a solo-patient room, with my own bathroom; visited daily by a cleaner, nurse, physiotherapist, and an occupational therapist.

Thirdly, being a solo-patient in this room, there was complete silence and serenity, which gave me the rare opportunity to read more religious books and lives of saints, aside from my daily prayers, as well as mass attendance through the television. I felt like I was on holidays!

Fourthly, this room had the perfect morning sun location! I had the chance of a lifetime, to watch the gorgeous morning star Venus set down and simultaneously, the glorious morning sun rise up and brighten the horizon! What an exceptional beauty! I was in total awe!

Thank You, O Lord for healing me and having holidays with You!

5. Giving Back God's Generosity

As a couple, Stephen and I truly appreciated God's love and generosity to us and our family. Through and through, we felt God's guidance and providence in our daily lives right through our children and their respective families. So, whenever there were opportunities to help those in need, we grabbed that moment, in order to repay God's goodness to us. In Stephen's side of family, we took that chance of sending two of his nieces to high school and later on, another two of his nieces to college. Likewise, on my family's side, we gladly sent two of my nieces and a cousin to college, as well as the young boy Rene whom I sent to school from elementary to high school, when I was still single. We believed that education is the best way of helping disadvantaged families. Education is the key to advancement and success, just like what was reflected in Stephen's life. At this present time, I am writing this book, three of them had finished their degrees and one will be graduating this year 2022.

Looking back, God gave us good earning jobs enough to support and provide for the essential needs of our family and with the extra hard-earned money through Stephen's overtime pay made it all possible to support our nieces with their college education. We heard some unpleasant comments from some people that we must be earning a lot of money which was how we could easily give support to the needy. We sadly heard negative comments like: "They were aspiring to be heroes that's why they help the poor and etc."

Poor souls! The more I felt sorry for this people with these kinds of harsh judgements and wrong notions. I always lifted them up to the Lord, to touch them and change their hearts!

Stephen and I sincerely gave back to God and will continue giving back to Him, His unending generosity and Divine Providence to us, by helping others following what He Himself said,

> *"Truly I say to you: whenever you did this to one of the least of my brothers and sisters, you did it to me." (Matthew 25:40)*

Chapter 10

Death in the Family

"For us, our citizenship is in heaven, from where we await the coming of our Saviour, Jesus Christ, the Lord. He will transform our lowly body, making it like His own body, radiant in glory, through the power which is His to subject everything to Himself." (Philippians 3:20-21)

1. My Family Ancestry's Short Lifespan

Tracing my ancestors' lifespan, I found out that they had short lifespan due to a genetic history of heart disease and hypertension. Tatay's side of family, like his siblings: Uncle Pablo, Aunt Angie, Uncle Nano, as well as their own father all died of heart attack in their early sixties and seventies.

My parents died so young, but their respective causes of death were different from our ancestral genetic history. Nanay died at the age of twenty-eight due to internal haemorrhage and Tatay died of lung cancer at the age of sixty-one.

Nanay suffered from heavy bleeding and thought that it was her first menstrual period after child birth, but was actually a miscarriage. Due to the remoteness of our village to doctors and hospitals, transport was a big challenge. I gathered from stories that my relatives struggled to get an ambulance. Everyone in the village was relieved when they finally heard the sound of an ambulance siren and rushed my poor mother 'bleeding to death' to the nearest hospital, but tragically, died on the way.

My father regularly worked in the city and home by the weekend with us. So, when this tragedy happened, he was in the city and received an emergency call to go home due to his wife's serious health condition. Because he knew how hard the transport was in our village, so, he hired an ambulance from the city to our place which was approximately one hundred and fifty kilometres away. As soon as he got home, it was too late, as Nanay has gone to her eternal home. I remembered very well that sombre night, when Tatay arrived, he loudly wept and hysterically wailed, called Nanay's name as he went up the fourteen steps of our two-storey house and there was Nanay's cold and lifeless body laid in her coffin. All the people present at that time cried bitterly too and felt so terribly sad for him, as a widower and also sad for all of us three children, as orphans, who lost our mother at such young ages. Liam was only one year old, I was only seven, and Kuya Nico was eight years old. It was so heartbreaking and traumatic for all of us, which up to this present time, I can still feel the pain and agony of that tragic, mournful and sorrowful night.

Tatay's lifestyle had changed for the worst, since Nanay passed away. He resorted to alcohol and drinking sessions on weekends just to forget his loneliness. He tried to move on with his life, so he married for the second time Nanay Julie and blessed with a daughter named Jade. But this marriage only lasted for two years and they separated. Nanay Julie left him due to his infidelities and vices. For so many years, Tatay became an alcoholic and a chain smoker. His lungs became weak, until he was diagnosed with lung cancer and sadly died at the age of sixty-one.

Kuya Nico, my eldest brother died also at an early age of fifty-eight due to a brain aneurysm, which is a bulge or ballooning in the brain's blood vessel that raptured. His bad habits of drinking alcohol and smoking aggravated his high blood pressure issues. As young as thirty-five years of age, he already suffered a mild stroke, and was able to luckily survive. Then, in his early forties, this treacherous disease struck him again. Through medications, he surpassed the critical period. Sadly, the third time he suffered a stroke, he died peacefully after forty-eight hours. So, Kuya Nico inherited our ancestral genetic history of heart disease and hypertension in his blood. Kuya Nico was only a year older than me, which is why I was also alarmed. So, I remained diligent to have a healthy life style like eating the right food, daily exercise and sunshine, faithful to medications, laugh a lot with my spouse, children, friends and most of all, have special and quality time of conversations with God.

Liam, my youngest brother died at the age of fifty-six. He did not survive his heart valve replacement. He was born with a very tiny tube in his aortic heart valve and sadly no one knew in the family, due to the absence of maternal care. With God's divine intervention, he grew up to be a very active child, until he became a basketball player during his teens. Liam was a talented and adventurous young man. Before we left our beloved motherland, we made sure that he had settled down. So, he got married and had three gorgeous children.

Because of his passion for greener pasture, he went to America and providentially became an independent home renovator. He successfully accomplished his dreams of rebuilding our ancestral home and the completion of his children's education. Unfortunately, when he reached the age of fifty-six, he started to struggle with his breathing and the only solution according to the specialist was a heart valve replacement. At this critical point in his life, Stephen and I decided to be with him in America, so we flew one week before his scheduled surgery. We lovingly spent quality time with him and stayed by his side until he was released from the hospital. Those were really precious and memorable moments in our lives, as we praised God for his successful operation! We returned back to Australia with peace and joy in my heart!

After twenty hours upon arrival to Australia, I was devastated when I received the shocking news about his death.

2. Who Can Comprehend God's will?

*J*ust right after our evening prayers, I sat down and sadly reminisced Liam's short life.

Last week of June 2016, I received a phone call from my youngest brother Liam from Chicago. I was so happy to talk to him and was able to catch up about our respective families. He did very well with his adventure in America as a home renovator. My cheerful mood was quickly changed into anxiety, when he told me about his urgent heart valve replacement. Without hesitation, Stephen and I booked our flight to be with him during his operation. I felt that it was the right thing to do as his elder sister. One week before his operation, we arrived in Chicago, and spent all the quality time together to see the beautiful place, his finished projects and on-going projects, and mainly we were able to catch up with his good and bad experiences as a resident worker in America. He did very well in his ten years working as a renovator. He was happy and proud to have been able to put this children through good schools until they finished and started to settle down with their own spouse and family. Most importantly, he was able to knockdown and rebuild our ancestral home, ruined by the eruption of Mount Pinatubo in 1991. I kept repeating to him these words: "Tatay in heaven must be so proud of your achievements. You were able to fulfill his dream of renovating our house. You did it magnificently much more than expected!" He was in tears every time I would utter these words to him.

Last week of August, before his scheduled operation, we prayed all together and Stephen led the prayers. I held his hands so tight and said, "God is with you and will never leave you!"

That night, I contemplated the meaning of my dream on the first week of June. I dreamt of a man lying on a bed. I couldn't see his face, but saw only his open chest and clearly saw his heart like a corroded iron! I was so emotionally affected by that dream and asked the Holy Spirit to give me His wisdom to understand its meaning. Until that last week of June, when I received a call from Liam. "Now, we are here Lord, that dream had clearly unfolded and it is alarming me to think about Liam. I totally surrender to you, my dear brother, that this surgery is a successful one. Please heal him, so he will be back to his normal life." Amen!

Very early in the morning, we were happily greeted by the surgeon who boasted of news of a successful operation! "Praise God!" The surgeon said. "It was just the right time for the operation. His heart valve was like a corroded iron, a valve meant for an eighty-year-old man!" I was shocked with the words uttered by the surgeon, which meant that Liam was the man in that dream. "Thank you, Lord for saving my brother!"

As soon as Liam was released from the hospital, Stephen and I flew back home. I felt so happy and peaceful and most of all praised and thanked God endlessly for His great Love to my brother!

We arrived safely and I rested my tired body after long hours of travel, but with a calm and peaceful spirit. I slept the whole day into night, until Stephen woke me up with shocking news! Liam was rushed back to the hospital due to severe chest pains and didn't make it to the hospital. I was shocked and devastated, as if the heavens had fallen on my head and asked the question, "Why Lord, Oh Why?" I wept and wailed bitterly. I was terribly shocked!

In the morning, we attended the Sunday mass with this question in my mind. My eyes were swollen because of tears that kept flowing until no more, but feelings of bitterness in my heart and restlessness of my soul. My heart stopped breathing when the reader proclaimed the Sunday's first reading from Wisdom 9:13-16,

"Indeed, who can know the intentions of God? Who can discern the plan of the Lord? For human reasoning is timid, and the plans of our minds are uncertain; a perishable body is a burden for the soul and our tent of clay weighs

down the active mind. We are barely able to know about the things of earth, and it is a struggle to understand what is close to us; who, then, can hope to understand heavenly things?"

While these words were being said, I was in tears again of the pain of guilt and fervently asked God's forgiveness for questioning and doubting Him. He is the God of All Knowing and Wisdom, therefore knows what is best for my brother. Oh! my Lord, forgive me! I am a sinner. Have mercy on me!

From then on, I was calm, peaceful and completely accepted the demise of Liam, who was now reunited happily with Kuya Nico, Tatay and Nanay in heaven! That was my perfect imagery, which gave my soul a feeling peace and joy!

3. How Do I View Death?

As a Christian who believes in heaven, hell and after life, death is an inspiration in aiming to live a productive and meaningful life. I clearly remembered my teacher Sister Agatha in my year two Religion class, who kept on repeating one question with one answer, every time we were in her class, "Why are you here on earth? You are here on earth: to know God, to love God, to serve God and to be with God in heaven." Eventually, I learned the true meaning and significance of her statements. Absolutely, these words were plunged in my heart and soul, which truly guided me in my spiritual journey.

Death is a reality that nobody can escape from; even the richest, famous and most powerful people are not spared from it. "Death comes like a thief in the night," as the common quotation states, which is very true. That's why, there is always the readiness in our minds, hearts and soul in order to be peaceful when it comes. Every opportunity or chance to hold onto our loved ones; to spend quality time with them, to forgive and forget grudges, set aside pettiness, and to show love and affection, should be grabbed right away!

Treat each day, as if it was our last!

Death is a motivation to be a person, with the good and right moral conduct, in preparation for the reward of eternal life in paradise. You may say that what I am saying is for preschool children only. In fact, I'd learned this fundamental Christian teaching from preschool, which later on in my adult life, found the truth behind it! Isn't this a perfect motivation to live a good life throughout our lives? If only people would have the same views, then this world would be a better and safer place to live in.

Why do people have a negative feeling towards death? One main reason is the fear of the unknown, that is, not knowing what happens after death. Other reasons are: not ready to leave loved ones, unfulfilled dreams and unpaid financial commitments.

From childhood, I have seen and experienced several passing of loved ones, most especially my mother. It was a huge blessing to be surrounded by religious sisters in removing my fear, and instilled in my mind, heart and soul the beauty of the place where my mother would be… in the Heavenly paradise with God, her eternal home. It is such a magnificent place, where everything is alluring, peaceful and serene! So, she must be in a beautiful place!

Then after 4 years, Aunt Nina, my father's sister who took good care of us three children, passed away too. I was 11 years old at that time, and felt extreme sadness, but not fear anymore, for I knew she will be with my mother in that peaceful, radiant paradise with God!

I became brave to face and accept death upon the passing of Tatay, Kuya Nico and Liam. I felt the same feelings of sadness of losing them, but mixed with the joy of glory knowing my loved ones are going home to their eternal abode with the Heavenly Father.

As I grew older, I'd learned to accept the fact that in dying we are born to eternal life, as shown in the following scriptural verses:

The Stoning to Death of Stephen – "When they heard these things, they were enraged and they gnashed their teeth at Stephen. But Stephen full of the Holy Spirit, gazed into heaven and saw the glory of God and Jesus at God's right hand. "Look!" he said, "I see the heavens opened and the Son of Man standing at the right hand of God." But they shouted and covered their ears with their hands, and rushed together upon him. They brought him out of the city and stoned him. The witnesses laid down their garments at the feet of a young man named Saul. As they were stoning him, Stephen prayed, "Lord Jesus, receive my spirit." Then he knelt down and said in a loud voice, "Lord, do not hold this sin against them," And when he had said this, he fell asleep." (Acts 7:54-59)

The Crucifixion – one of the criminals asking God's forgiveness, "Turning to Jesus, he said,

"Jesus, remember me when you come into your kingdom." Jesus replied, "Truly I tell you, today you will be with me in Paradise." (Luke 23:42-43)

The Death of Jesus – "It was now about noon. The sun was hidden and darkness came over the whole land until the ninth hour; and at that time the curtain of the Sanctuary was torn into two. Then Jesus gave a loud cry, "Father, into your hands, I commend my spirit." And saying that, he gave up his spirit." (Luke 23:44-46)

Death comes one day and the good news is that, it is not the end. We have hope for salvation and eternal life into His Heavenly paradise through Jesus Christ. Amen!

Chapter 11

Travels and "Holydays" with God

"Know that the Lord is God; He created us, and we belong to Him, we are His people, the sheep of His fold. Enter His gates with thanksgiving, and His courts with praise; give thanks to Him and bless His name. For the Lord is good and His love lasts forever, and His faithfulness through all generations." (Psalm 100:3-5)

1. Bucket Lists Before Retirement

2011-2021

At the onset of the year 2011, Stephen and I wrote down our bucket lists before our retirement within a ten-year period. Our main priority was to travel to different religious places tracing the Holy Life of Jesus Christ in Israel, the Evangelisation of Saint Paul, and the different apparition sites in the world of Blessed Virgin Mother Mary, including her humble house in Ephesus, Turkey. We never thought of visiting Las Vegas or New York or even the famous Disneyland. Our goal was to travel and have holydays with the Lord, Mother Mary and Saint Paul!

We remembered very well the words of one financial adviser, "It is very wrong to plan your travels after retirement! I often hear people saying that they will travel the world when they retire. It is a big mistake! First of all, when you spend money out, there is no more coming in, because you're not working anymore. Secondly, you might have some health issues by that time, like struggles with walking, or some restrictions, which would surely lessen your full enjoyment. So, plan your travels, while you're young and working!"

Indeed! Very true and we followed his words of financial guidance and wisdom. As soon as Ben and Lara, our couple-leaders from Couples for Christ community informed us that they had organised a Holy Land Pilgrimage Tour, we immediately expressed our willingness to join the tour. They had organised this tour for CFC members, relatives and friends and scheduled in October 2011. It was a perfect month, as we have ample time to save up for the airfares. What made it so easy and convenient for the forty-two pilgrims who signed up for the forthcoming pilgrimage tour was the three-payment plan.

First, was the ten percent deposit, second, the half payment of the balance and third, the last full payment.

Fortunately, by July we will receive tax refunds from the government. So, indeed it helped a lot in making this dream a reality!

a. Holy Land Pilgrimage Tours – 2011

On the 22nd of October 2011, we flew from Sydney to Bangkok for an overnight stopover and proceeded on the following day to Tel Aviv, Israel. I had goosebumps all over, as we entered Jerusalem that very first night and heard the classical sweet-sounding song 'Jerusalem' when the driver dramatically put it on. We all had tears in our eyes, for at that very moment we were all still in ecstasy of this privilege of just being there in the Holy Land of Jesus! It was an indescribable feeling of joy and peace in our hearts! I was in awe!

The following day, after morning prayers led by our spiritual chaplain, we started our tour around Jerusalem. It was a lifetime experience to see in front of our eyes the traces of Jesus' pain and agony when we visited Golgotha, the exact place where He was excruciatingly crucified. Then the next day's schedule made us all eager and excited to view Jesus' burial site and tomb.

There in the Holy Land of Jesus, I noticed that all pilgrims regarded each other as brothers and sisters regardless of race, gender and religion. Every pilgrim respected each other's beliefs and faith. There are only three major religious beliefs there: Judaism, Islam and Christianity, as explained to us by our tour guide.

Thousands of pilgrims from different parts of the world queued at the burial site, so we woke up as early as four o'clock in the morning, in order to beat the long queue. Through persistence, we were able to be at the holiest site, the tomb of Jesus! I was in awe, most especially when I knelt in front of the tomb and touched even only the cord line, for there was a two-metre distance to the site. Oh, Lord Jesus, have mercy on me!

Everyone had an awesome experience during the renewal of marriage vows at Cana, which was solemnly officiated by the priest and gave each couple a renewal certificate. This was the exact site where Jesus attended a wedding feast and unexpectedly, the host ran out of wine. Jesus saved them from embarrassment upon the request of His beloved Mother Mary and He performed His first miracle of changing water into wine!

Stephen and I felt so blessed, as we celebrated our 35th wedding anniversary that year, in this memorable wedding site of Jesus' first miracle! What an honour and humbling experience! We eagerly continued our tour without complaints of the heat or struggles with walking or even hunger, as long as we had bottled water with us. The next site was to view the panoramic vista of the Mount of Beatitudes and the Sea of

Galilee. There, I felt refreshed with the serenity and calmness of the holy place surrounded by palm trees and olive trees. My body and soul gained inner peace and indescribable joy, which will be cherished all my life!

Another overwhelming experience during the Holy Land Pilgrimage was the boat ride on the Sea of Galilea. I envisioned Jesus was with us, facing the sea and His hands raised up to the heavens, while all pilgrims were in meditations and reflections with songs of praises!

We had a special tour to the fourteen stations and the Via Dolorosa, and visited the Church of the Holy Sepulchre, then proceeded to the Church of Saint Anne, marking the holy place of birth of the Blessed Mother.

Our experience of baptism at the river Jordan was unforgettable, re-committed to the rites of baptism, submerged in water at the very site where John the Baptist baptised Jesus! It was indeed an incredible experience of a lifetime! We praise and thank You, Oh Lord God!

The last part of the tour was the incredible swim in the Dead Sea, where everyone floated!

Why? The dead sea's salt concentration is too high making the water very dense, that's why humans float in the dead sea, as explained to us by our tour guide! So, we all tried it and experienced this unbelievable scientific fact! He also added that there was no fish there, because they won't survive the salt water, but has health benefits to humans. The water's mineral and low allergen content such as calcium and potassium has been found beneficial to human skin to stay young and healthy. Which is why the Dead Sea became a famous tourist site for people with skin issues. Rich and famous people visit that place annually as their holiday destination mainly for health and therapeutic benefits. Wow! Incredible! Praise God and Your magnificent creations!

As we prepared for our departure next day, we ended the night with a Thanksgiving Mass, expressing all our praises and thanksgiving to our Heavenly Father for making this Pilgrimage possible! Stephen and I suddenly realised that truly this remarkable tour manifested God's guidance to us, to primarily 'come home' to His Holy place on the exact date of October 22, 1988, twenty-three years after leaving our own beloved motherland; come home to the historical place and birth of our Faith!

Tears of joy flowed down our cheeks and we endlessly thanked God! Indeed, this was an unforgettable experience to each and every one of us! Praise to You, Oh Lord God!

b. Marian and Miracle Sites of Faith Pilgrimage Tours – 2014

Stephen and I attended the evening mass of the Feast of Assumption of the Virgin Mary, which is regarded as a holy day of obligation by Catholics. In the Catholic Church, the faithful are expected to attend Mass and refrain from heavy work. I was so deeply inspired to travel and visit the traces of Virgin Mary's apparitions in different parts of the world.

That night, I dreamt that we were in a car with our couple leaders, Ben and Lara, traveling a very long downhill and uphill and winding roads looking for a particular church. We felt we were lost, so we stopped and politely asked an old man walking on the side of the rugged road with a wide brimmed hat protecting himself from the soaring heat of the sun. With a smile on his face, he gently said, "Follow this road, then turn left three times, and you will see the church." Finally, we saw the church from a distance! One focal point of the dream was the part when I saw the Blessed Mother seated with a golden crown on her head!

That weekend, during our prayer meeting with Ben and Lara, I shared with them my dream and our eagerness once again to join a Marian Tour, in case they were planning another pilgrimage. My heart leapt with joy, when they said, "Next year 2014, let's mark our calendars for September, being the birth month of Our Blessed Mother Mary, we will explore and visit her apparition sites in Europe!" Amen!

There were fifteen pilgrims who enthusiastically committed to join the Marian Pilgrimage, scheduled on September 8 – 24, 2014 visiting the Marian and Miracle Sites in Italy, Spain, Portugal and France. I looked forward to see the realisation and fruition of my significant dream that night, where I vividly saw Blessed Mother Mary's golden crown!

Days and months quickly had passed and I couldn't believe that we were scheduled to fly to Dubai the following night, then to Rome, as our first destination! The prestigious Travel and Tours' director Marie met us for lunch at Makati, Manila. She generously hosted the sumptuous lunch, and afterwards distributed our respective tickets and gave us her final instructions for tomorrow's flight.

Rome, was our first stop, the capital and centre of the metropolitan city of Italy, known for its stunning architecture, the Colosseum, Pantheon, and Trevi Fountain as the main attractions. This is where the smallest country in the world can be found, the Vatican City!

At the Vatican City, we were blessed to secure the front section for the Audience with the Pope and attended mass which he officiated with many other Cardinals concelebrated with him. That was an awesome feeling to be in this holy and sacred place celebrating the Holy Eucharist with the Head of the Church and thousands and thousands of pilgrims all over the world! Praise God!

We proceeded to see the famous Sistine Chapel with its magnificent frescoes depicting the "Last Judgement" by Michaelangelo and other beautiful paintings of the masters. We went underground to the tombs of the Popes.

Italy is famous for the religious site of Saint Pio's birthplace at Pietrelcina and the "Home for the Relief of Suffering," a well-known charitable work founded by a stigmatist priest, popularly known as Padre Pio in 1920. Millions of pilgrims annually visit this hospital where he stayed and died in 1968 at the age of 81. He was canonised as Saint Pio in 2002 at Saint Peter's Square, Vatican City by Pope John Paul II. This hospital in San Giovanni Rotondo, Italy is now administered by Vatican City.

Of course, the tour wouldn't be complete without visiting the incredible "Leaning Tower of Pisa," the campanile, or free-standing bell tower, which withstood the test of time and ages with its imperfect leaning position of nearly a four-degree lean, without collapsing!

In Spain, we visited the famous "Sagrada Familia" a one-of-a-kind temple for its origins in foundation and purposes, and later on turned into a Basilica designed by a genius architect Antoni Gaudi. His work on the building is part of a UNESCO World Heritage Site.

Then, I was so excited to see the famous religious site in Spain, The Black Virgin, "Virgin Morenata" of Monserrat, Barcelona. We drove passed endless and breathtaking serrated mountains, until we reached the Benedictine monastery which houses an ancient wooden statue of the Black Virgin and Child Jesus. This was the point where my dream of seeing the Virgin Mary seated with a golden crown on her head, was revealed! All pilgrims had to queue to venerate and kneel in front of the

Blessed Virgin's statue. On my turn, I was in tears of joy to see her with the golden crown on her head! This was in reality, not a dream!

Portugal was the next country to visit, with the main focus on the miraculous apparition site of Our Lady of Fatima, where she appeared to the three shepherd-children namely: Lucia, Francisco and Jacinta. We had reached the religious site at night and blest to attend a solemn candle light procession, while praying the rosary. Again, thousands of pilgrims filled the huge and spacious area of the famous Shrine!

I looked forward to see the next miraculous Shrine of Our Lady of Lourdes, the sacred site where the Blessed Mother appeared to Bernadette, a young sickly and frail fourteen-year-old-girl and asked for a chapel to be built at the nearby cave grotto. There appeared a spring of healing water, attested by many pilgrims who drank the water and bathed in the spring, that they were miraculously healed.

We arrived at night in our assigned hotel which was about 1.5 kms to the Shrine of Our Lady. The tour guide told us to have dinner and after an hour, we will all walk to the shrine.

While we were walking, I remembered my dream on the night of August 15 last year, about three left turns going to a church. Right there, we just had our last third left turn and there, we were at the entry of the Shrine and welcomed by a Huge Golden Crown! Again, part of my dream was revealed in this holy and sacred place! Oh, thank You Lord for this blessing!

I slept with an overwhelming happiness, peace and contentment in my heart!

After a last look of Paris' famous Eiffel Tower, we proceeded to Montmartre's Sacre Coeur Church, inspired by the Sacred Heart Devotion of Saint Margaret Mary Alcoque which began in Paray-Le-Monial. The following day, we visited the Great Basilica of the Carmelite Convent at Lisieux dedicated to Saint Therese the Little Flower of Jesus, who was canonised by Pope Pius XI in 1925 and was the youngest person to be designated a doctor of the church. The collection of her essays conveys her loving pursuit of holiness in ordinary life, and thus defined her doctrine of the Little Way, the way of trust and absolute surrender to God's ways and will.

We were nearly at the end of the tour, but it wouldn't be complete without visiting the famous Louvre Museum, where we saw the magnificent works of art, including the original painting of the Mona Lisa. We ended the day at the Chapel of the Miraculous Medal in Rue de Bac, where the incorrupt body of Saint Catherine Laboure is still lying-in state. This medal of the Immaculate Conception is more popularly known as the Miraculous Medal, which was designed by the Blessed Virgin Mary who manifested the design to a young novice Catherine Laboure of the Daughters of Charity in the Chapel of the Motherhouse.

The devotees believed that those who wear it will receive great graces, especially if they wear it around the neck, and at the same time under the protection of the Mother of God.

Everyone was tired physically after a full day's activities, but extremely filled in spirit of peace, joy and love at the culmination of these life-changing and rich experiences we gained in this Voyage to the Marian and Miracle Sites of Faith! Praise the Lord!

c. Steps of Saint Paul – 2016

*M*id-year of 2015, the local Travel and Tours company sent out brochures of another pilgrimage, called Steps of Saint Paul, which was the next noted travel plan in our bucket list. Both Stephen and I were so excited to hear from Marie the director, who was expected to arrive in Sydney that weekend. We really endeavoured to see her, in order to confirm our genuine interest to join the tour. She gave us a big surprise! The following year in 2016, their famous and prestigious company will be celebrating its 20th anniversary in the field of travel and tours, so, they were giving twenty percent discount of the total package deal as a promotion! We were happy with the total amount! So, we signed up straight away and gave her our ten per cent deposit. The tour was confirmed to be on April 09 – May 02, 2016.

Due to some political unrest at the beginning of the year 2016, we, as the pilgrims included this trip in our everyday prayers that everything will go through smoothly before, during and after the trip! There were several instances as shown in the news of unrest and bombings in the Middle East and some parts of the world. So, it was a bit alarming to travel at this period, particularly in Turkey. In fact, some of the members of the group actually pulled out because of the fear of terrorist attack and civil war! I asked Stephen's opinion if we too will have to make the same decision to pull out. Without fear, he said, "If we die, it's such an honour to be in a pilgrimage!" What a man of strong conviction and deep faith towards God's love and majestic power! I absolutely agreed with him and felt peace and joy in my heart.

In February 2016, I dreamed of a spacious arena, filled with people singing and praising God all their might! A very powerful voice reverberated through the huge arena coming from a very passionate speaker. Then, followed by the fellowship of brothers and sisters from a group happily chatting while enjoying the different kinds of food being sold in food stalls. I saw a multitude of people of different nationalities gathered together, but in groups identified through a placard or banner revealing what country they came from! What a vibrant and colourful picture!

I woke up in awe! I was so happy to see such scenario of people gathered with one faith!

I instantly knew that my dream was about the forthcoming pilgrimage in the next two months. Due to my excitement and enthusiasm to see and trace the evangelical path of Saint Paul, that even in my sleep this passion was clearly manifested.

This pilgrimage tour will lead us to Saint Paul's Ministry of Evangelisation, spreading the good news in different parts of Greece, Turkey and Malta. I had this utmost enthusiasm of also visiting the humble dwelling of our Blessed Virgin in Turkey! I couldn't wait for that memorable day! My memory took me back to the words of the dying Jesus on the cross when He uttered the words, "Woman, here is your son." Then He said to the disciple, "Here is your mother." (John 19:26-27) From then on, the beloved apostle John took with him the Blessed Mother Mary to his place in Turkey.

Finally, in April 2016, our group tour left Australia and landed safely in Greece. The very next day, we eagerly started the day with prayers led by our Spiritual Director Fr. Alan and headed to Philippi. I was in awe kneeling in front of the Baptistry Chapel in honour of Lydia, the first woman evangelised and baptised by Saint Paul, who offered her dwelling as an assembly place for meetings of the faithful. She was a woman of means, a seller of purple cloth and known for her hospitality and generosity during the evangelistic days of Saint Paul.

Here in Philippi, I was stunned into silence and felt goosebumps when we started walking on the well-paved roads, formerly rugged-rocky-dusty roads, which left traces of

Saint Paul's steps on these roads, together with his followers. I couldn't believe that I was literally walking on the path he took approximately 49-51 AD! I felt so overwhelmed and contentedly took this as the apex or culmination of our tour!

Then, the tour guide led us to the prison site, where Paul and Silas were arrested, flogged and imprisoned for causing a public nuisance. As narrated by the tour guide, while in prison, they sat with their feet in stocks singing hymns, until at midnight, an earthquake broke open the prison doors, setting the prisoners free. Horribly terrified, the jailer feared that his superiors would blame him for the jail break, he prepared to run himself through with a sword rather than face the punishment. Paul and Silas convinced him not to harm himself; they preached the Gospel to him, and he was saved, along with his household that night and were converted to Christianity!

Then we headed to Thessalonica, where Paul preached at the synagogues. There were hundreds and hundreds of pilgrims at the synagogues we visited, singing and praising God (the same as what I saw in my dream). We joined them and followed what they were doing.

Then, the priest blest an icon of Saint Paul stating "The Preacher-Evangeliser for Christ" and all the pilgrims, including us clapped our hands likened to a "standing ovation" and ended the liturgy with the sign of the cross. Outside the synagogue, there were some people selling all kinds of snacks for the pilgrims at the same time greeting each other as brothers and sisters in the same faith (again same as in my dream).

Wow! I was in awe because I remembered that dream of a "spacious arena, filled with people singing and praising God" was right there in front of me!

"A powerful voice reverberated in the huge arena coming from a passionate speaker" was no other than Saint Paul himself. He was fearless, bold and daring, for he believed God called him, therefore, He will be with him always.

We drove along the beautiful seaside town of Alexandroupolis, then crossed the Greek and Turkish borders and enjoyed a full day tour to Gallipoli Anzac Battle fields, Anzac Cove and Lone Pine remembering the brave men who lost their lives in the Battle of Gallipoli.

Then, we proceeded to Istanbul, the city which connects the East and West. Our first stop was the Blue Mosque, the most famous in both Turkish and Islamic world, the only mosque built with six minarets and decorated with famous Iznik tiles. Then, we visited Saint Sophia Museum, the largest imperial church in the city built by Constantine in the 4th century, which today is regarded as a magnificent monument representing the influence of two religions: Islam and Christianity.

This part of the tour truly amazed me! By private boat, we cruised along the Bosphorus Strait, a winding strait separating Europe and Asia. Behind us, we left Europe and entered along the shores of Asia Minor with its delightful mixture of the past and present, its grand splendour and beauty of modern hotels, palaces, fortresses and small fishing villages. We visited the most impressive biblical site of our trip: Ephesus, the place where Paul visited three times and stayed two years preaching, evangelising and where special miracles were wrought! Then we proceeded further into inner Turkey, and finally went to my most-awaited part of the tour - The House of the Virgin Mary, a Catholic shrine located on Mt. Koressos in the vicinity of Ephesus, seven kilometres from Selquk/Izmir in Turkey. It was indeed an indescribable feeling to be inside the humble house of our Blessed Mother Mary!

I was in total ecstasy, as I imagined the Blessed Mother bowed down on her knees, humbly praying alone and hugging a crucifix close to her heart! I felt tears flowing down my cheeks, while giving praises and thanksgiving to our Lord God Almighty!

We embarked our cruise ship at noon and arrived in the early afternoon on the island of Patmos, considered a holy island of the Christian religion, where John the Divine was exiled and wrote the Apocalyptic Revelations, which constitute the last part of the New Testament.

The cruise continued on a leisure trip to the volcanic island of Santorini, took the cable car to visit the top of the island and enjoyed the breathtaking panoramic view of the famous Caldera, which is a large volcanic crater, formed by a major eruption leading to the collapse of the volcano's mouth.

The last leg of our tour was Malta, a small country with three islands. As we landed, the tour guide drove us to Medina to visit Saint Paul's Church, catacombs and the Grotto where Saint Paul is said to have lived and preached after his shipwreck. Then, he drove us to Saint Paul's Bay, where the apostle came ashore after being shipwrecked. We walked to the famous fountain called Ghajin Razul (the Apostle's Fountain), where Saint Paul struck a rock which is said to have miraculously brought water. In the afternoon, we drove to Valetta, the capital of Malta, where we visited Saint Paul's Shipwreck Church, one of the oldest churches in Valetta and viewed the vault paintings of Attilio Palumbo, portraying the episodes of Saint Paul's life, as well as the two most important relics, an arm bone of Saint Paul and a piece of the column which he was beheaded. This memorable day ended with the visit to Saint John's Cathedral, wherein Caravaggio's masterpiece, 'The Beheading of John the Baptist' hangs in the oratory!

Truly remarkable, we saw the paths of martyrdom and sainthood because of strong conviction, love, and faith in God! It was indeed, unimaginable and incomprehensible the ways and methods of death of these saints and martyrs, who tremendously suffered to defend their intense belief in Christ's teachings!

The final day of our tour in Malta was a leisure day of visiting well known outlets of gold-plated and silver-plated jewels such as rings, bracelets, necklaces and earrings. Then, surprisingly, the tour guide generously added a bonus trip to Mosta at the Church of the Assumption of Our Lady, a city in central Malta, because we still had the time to visit the historical place, where a miracle happened! I felt so excited and extremely curious, so I stayed closer to the tour guide, so I could hear all what he had to say. On April 9, 1942, two German bombs fell on the Church, while Mass was going on at the time and more than 250 parishioners were in the Church. Alarms rang out, some people left the church and others stayed inside and fervently prayed to God for shield and protection. This old Church built between 1833 and 1860 was saved from destruction, as well as the faithful parishioners inside spared from death because the bombs miraculously didn't explode!

Indeed, another manifestation of God's power and triumph over darkness! Praise God!

Then, I curiously asked, "What happened to the bombs?" The tour guide continued his story that the bombs were hastily defused by the military and later dropped into the sea. They made a replica of the bomb which we saw on display at the back of the church, as a constant reminder on the historic and remarkable day, when God showed His divine intervention and great love to His people!

Thank you! Oh Lord God, for leading us to this life changing experience!

d. Graces of Eastern Europe – 2019

Since the Steps of Saint Paul's tour in April 2016, there were series of challenges that happened in our family. Within the year of 2016, both sides of our families painfully experienced deaths of loved ones.

First of September, just after five months upon arrival, shocked and heart-broken, my youngest brother Liam passed away. Then after three months, December 5, sadly, my best friend and sister-in-law Leni died. Just after nine days, December 13, Stephen's mother grievously passed away too. What I had seen and experienced during our pilgrimage during the year, had absolutely deepened my faith and trust in the Lord, and made me stronger and more resilient during the troubled and grieving times.

June 2019, Stephen had a health scare. While at work, he was rushed to the nearest hospital, as soon as his workmates saw him go very pale and weak. Then the hospital doctor gave him a letter to our family doctor to continue with a series of test relating to heart issues. For two months, Stephen faithfully followed all the necessary medical procedures and instructions given to him by the doctors and specialist, for he desperately wanted to be back to his normal health. We both fervently prayed to God to have all the series of tests resulting to all positive directions towards his full recovery.

A month prior to Stephen's health scare, we submitted our names to join the Pilgrimage of the Graces of Eastern Europe this coming October 2019. That's why, we both ardently prayed for good test results, so we can join this pilgrimage, which marks our last leg in our travel's bucket list before retirement.

After long and arduous two months of prayers and novenas for the good results of Stephen's test, God once again, manifested His great love to us! Amazingly, he was given a clearance to travel by our family doctor. Praise God for Your Majestic Power!

On October 13, 2019, a group of sixteen pilgrims, including the Spiritual Director arrived in Dubai and took a connecting flight to Frankfurt, Germany. Upon arrival, we were met by the tour director who led us to the major sites of the city like the 'Florence of the Elbe' in Dresden, the former capital of Saxony in the Elbe River. Then explored on foot the Zwinger and the Semper Opera House to the Royal Palace which was under reconstruction. We crossed the mighty river Elbe to visit Wittenberg, where in 1517, Martin Luther nailed his 95 theses to the door of Schlosskirche and set the Reformation in motion. This is the site where Luther himself lies buried in the same church.

The following day, the tour guide led us to Czech Republic and visited Saint Vitus Cathedral with its grand chapel studded with semi-precious stones, the Basilica of Saint George and the Church of Our Lady of Victorious, where the image of the Infant Jesus (Sto. Nino de Praga) is enshrined. I was in awe in every church we went in and felt tremendously blest to be in these sacred places!

The next in our itinerary was the visit to Poland's famous Jasna Gora Sanctuary in Czestochowa, home to the cherished miraculous Icon of Our Lady with the Child Jesus, an object of veneration for centuries and also known as the Black Madonna. Our Lady of Czestochowa is recognised as one of the most visited places of Christian pilgrimage in the world and attracts approximately five million pilgrims every year. This was one of my most desired Marian sites to visit and venerate and so blessed that it did come into fruition!

The next day was a trip that I didn't really want to visit, but I had to see it and be brave.

I had this bitter feeling of great sorrow, when I saw this 'Golgotha of the modern world,' as termed by Saint John Paul II which was the biggest concentration camp of Hitler's Nazism in Auschwitz. That camp horribly put to death millions of Jews through the gas chambers. It was a very depressing place, as if I could hear the wailing and groaning in pains of the victims from a sadistic and vicious man who had fallen into the deepest pit of darkness of greed and evil doings! All of us, as a group led by the tour leader prayed for all the souls of those who suffered and died there, that their souls rest in peace.

The next stop for the day was certainly the contrary to the atmosphere of this morning's trip. I looked forward to see the birthplace of Karol Wojtyla, the real name of Saint John Paul

II in Wadowice. We visited his family home and saw his own room as well as the grounds where he played football, followed by a visit to the Parish Church to see the famous Baptismal basin where Karol was baptised.

The next itinerary was the visit to the famous Shrine of Divine Mercy in Krakow, Poland.

Here stands the chapel of the miraculous image of Merciful Jesus and the sacred tomb of Saint Faustina in her incorruptible body. It was indeed a blessed and solemn day which culminated with a thanksgiving mass!

The group departed towards south and crossed into the Slovakian Republic through a magnificent alpine landscape into Hungary, enroute to the beautiful city of Budapest.

Situated on the opposite bank of the Danube, the former cities of Buda and Pest are linked by a series of graceful bridges. I enjoyed the magnificent and enchanting Budapest at night with its gorgeous colours which accentuated the grandiose architectural beauty of palaces and citadels. It was a very remarkable and beautiful night, like that of a fairyland!

Finally, the group departed for Medjugorje, a place of prayer and reflection and experienced the beauty and peace of this simple village, where Our Lady of Queen of Peace appeared to visionaries in 1981, now called Apparition Hill, a two kilometres climb through rocks and boulders from central Medjugorje to the top of the Hill. That was not an easy climb, but anyone who persists and endures eventually reached the top victoriously! I was able to climb it with the help and support of Stephen! To me, that was the main highlight of that pilgrimage! What an unforgettable and triumphant experience! I praise and thank You Lord!

The next day's trip was another big surprise! The group travelled to Slovenia going to Bled to visit the famous Church of the Assumption, which is located in the middle of Lake Bled.

Upon arrival in Bled, we took a boat ride to the Church with 99 steps before reaching the Church itself for reflections and prayers. This Church too is famous for its "wishing bells" wherein the visitors had the chance to ring the bell by pulling the heavy ropes. The story says, that ringing it, can make your secret wishes come true! All of us gladly participated in ringing the 'wishing bells,' with expectant faith that our prayers will be answered in God's time and His ways. We left the Church with peace and joy in our hearts!

Then we took a private tour to Bled Castle, one of the most famous tourist attractions in Slovenia, built on top of a 130-metre cliff overlooking Lake Bled. It was such a superb and magnificent view day and night!

This pilgrimage tour culminated in the wonderful city of Vienna, where we visited Saint Stephen Cathedral and Our Lady of Bowed Head and had our Thanksgiving Mass. Then proceeded to the famous Schonbrunn Palace, the official summer residence in modern Vienna and enjoyed the magnificent and artistic landscape of gardens and different varieties of colourful flowers! Then we were given two hours last minute shopping, followed by dinner then immediate transfer to the airport for evening flight back home!

Thank you, Oh Lord God Almighty for blessing us this astonishing and memorable pilgrimage to the Graces of Eastern Europe!

Overwhelmed, Stephen and I were able to fulfill the completion of our travel's bucket list:

Holydays with Jesus, Mother Mary and Saint Paul! Praise God! Amen! Amen! Amen!

2. Travel Missions Accomplished through God's Providence

From the very beginning of our marriage, Stephen and I had experienced endless graces and blessings from God. We felt the hands of God guiding us in the right direction and we obediently followed the flow of the river to wherever He led us.

Regarding our travels and holydays, both of us thought of the same goal. We loved to see and explore the places where faith all begun in the life of Jesus in the Holy Land of Israel, then followed by the apparition sites of the Blessed Virgin Mary and the traces of the steps of Saint Paul. With all of these in mind, Stephen and I really worked hard to save up for the first on the list – Holy Land Pilgrimage Tour. In all our personal prayers, Masses and Novenas, this intention was constantly included.

Much to our surprise, the remaining balance of our trip was easily paid off through our tax refund on the 2011 financial year end. So, the first pilgrimage was successfully completed in October 22 – 2 November 2011. This pilgrimage had tremendously touched both of us! We felt honoured and privileged to witness the holy places from where Jesus was born till His excruciating death, which is regarded as one of the most defining moments in human history! Another very precious and cherished moment was our renewal of marriage vows at the site where Jesus performed His very first miracle of changing water into wine in the wedding feast in Cana, Galilee! Our renewal of marriage vows timely marked our 35th wedding anniversary. It was such a valued and treasured moment in our lives! Praise God!

The second pilgrimage was: A Special Voyage to the Marian and Miracle Sites of Faith. This tour came into fruition from my dream on the Feast of Assumption of the Virgin Mary in August 15, 2013. True enough, it all happened through God's blessings! We had the precious pilgrimage on September 8-24, 2014. Almost all of what I had seen in my dream unfolded when we visited the different places, especially at the Shrine of Lourdes in France and The Black Virgin in Monserrat, Barcelona!

Again, God gave us His divine providence in financial support to this beloved pilgrimage.

Stephen received a redundancy package from his company and secured another employment after one week out of work! His package is more than enough to fund our next pilgrimages! God manifested His great generosity upon us. "For of His fullness we have all received, grace upon grace." (John 1:16)

The third pilgrimage was: The Steps of Saint Paul. This much awaited pilgrimage came into realisation in April 09 - May 02, 2016. It was a huge concern due to the bombings of Istanbul, Turkey two weeks before the departure. I asked Stephen if we're still going ahead with the plan. I was so impressed with his answer, "It's such an honour to die in a pilgrimage!"

Indeed, very true! So, we went ahead as scheduled, though many of the pilgrims pulled out from the tour, and the tour operators still continued the trip as planned. True to God's promise of protection, we came home safe and sound! "Be valiant and strong, do not fear or tremble before them, for the Lord your God is with you, He will not leave you or abandon you." (Deuteronomy 31:6)

The fourth and last pilgrimage tour, listed in our bucket list was: The Graces of Eastern Europe scheduled on October 12-27, 2019. I really looked forward to this pilgrimage mainly because of the well-known challenge in climbing the Apparition Hill in Medjugorje, Bosnia.

Again, God is forever good! The last company which hired Stephen had outsourced the workers to another local company and he was one of them. This heightened our happiness, because this blessing of another redundancy was more than enough to fund our last pilgrimage tour!

Stephen successfully got into a casual job in 2018. He enjoyed his work and most of all went along very well with his work mates. Until an alarming incident occurred in June 2019,

Stephen was rushed to the hospital by his work supervisor due to breathing difficulty. He was impelled to undergo lots of test to be done within two months, which made me think that we won't be able to join the next and last pilgrimage.

We prayed fervently for good results and asked Mother Mary's intercession in this petition.

For the meantime, Stephen patiently and diligently followed all the doctor's instructions and recommendations. With God's graces of healing, Stephen was rewarded with good results from all his tests! He was miraculously blest with the quick recovery from sickness, as if nothing had happened to him! Truly, God manifested upon us His divine providence and protection in order to accomplish our last pilgrimage tour and holydays with the Lord!

Thank you, Oh Lord, my God Almighty! Praise and exalt Your holy name forever! Amen!

> *"If you serve the lord, your God, He will bless your food and your water, and I will keep sickness away from you." (Exodus 23:25)*

"The Lord, the God of his father David says: I have heard your prayer and I have seen your tears. And now I will cure you. On the third day, you will go up to the House of the Lord." (2 Kings 20:5)

Chapter 12

The Glory of Retirement

"Whatever you do, do it wholeheartedly, working for the Lord, and not for human masters. For you know well that the Lord will reward you with the inheritance. You are servants, but your Lord is Christ. Every evil doer will be paid back for whatever wrong he has done, for God does not make exceptions in favour of anyone." (Colossians 3:23-25)

1. God said, "It's Time to Retire."

May 2020

As soon as Stephen and I arrived in the first week of November 2019 from our last pilgrimage in Eastern Europe, the whole world initially faced the most challenging health scare, which was the fast and furious spread of a virus called Covid 19. This virus continued to spread and produce variants up to this present time as I write this book. Almost five million people around the world have died from this fatal virus.

From our tour, our lives changed dramatically. Stephen worked at a cold storage of dairy products in one main distribution centre in Sydney. Because of the presence of chronic bronchitis in his last diagnosis, he wasn't given clearance to work by our family doctor. Being a workaholic, he did his best to recover and be back to his normal health. He informed his supervisor to give him another month to get well, even leave without pay. After one month, he went back to our family doctor and sadly, he wasn't given the 'green light' to work in the cold storage, unless he could be transferred to another department with normal room temperature. I saw his face go red and he looked devastated! I felt so sorry for Stephen and suggested that we visit and pay homage to the Blessed Sacrament in the nearby church and pray for God's guidance. I saw his face glow with radiance of peace and joy when we left the church, but he was still quiet and didn't say a word. At night, we prayed our usual seven o'clock rosary and peacefully went to bed.

The sky was so blue and bright the next day's glorious morning and Stephen woke up thanking and praising the Lord for His message to him through his dream! He told me, God said, "It's time to retire!" He was in tears and kept repeating that he heard God's voice telling him to retire and fully serve Him. So, finally in May 2020, he was officially retired!

Turning seventy years old this year 2020, retirement is already long overdue, right? Our children kept reminding their Dad about retirement, which he just ignored. Now, God Himself told him so and he gladly obeyed!

At work, I was the first employee sent home by my new manager to work from home, being the most senior in our administration department. This was absolutely convenient for me, as it meant no more driving to work. My manager was aware of my husband's health condition, so he knew I preferred to be at home. From that day on, it was like a practice or conditioning for Stephen and I, if we could survive being together 24/7. I had heard, as well as witnessed stories about marriage break-ups upon retirement, for the couple couldn't stand being with each other for twenty-four hours, seven days a week! I checked and analysed our very own relationship and found out that it may not be perfect, but manageable in a very loving and gentle way!

The secret is: CPSST which stands for Communicate, Pray, Serve, and Stay Together.

At the end of May 2020, my manager called me through a Zoom meeting and unexpectedly I received the greatest surprise and gift: notice for retirement effective the end of June 2020 with an abundance of blessings unimaginable! I was over the moon and tears of joy flowed freely down my cheeks, as I knelt down, prayed and shouted with joy and thanksgiving for God's endless providential love and care upon us! We praise and thank You, Oh Lord God Almighty, King of Kings and Lord of Lords! Amen!

2. Have Goals Set Before Your Retirement

So many stories I've heard of some retirees, who went back to work after a few months because of boredom due to lack of daily activities. A famous speaker about retirement gave one basic advice to those nearly reaching retirement age: Set your goals, and then plan your activities.

I was a bit puzzled upon hearing such stories of boredom, for I didn't see myself in the same situation. I had already set my long-term goals and I definitely knew what I wanted to do.

Number one on my list is to be a Catechist in the state schools of our parish in order to teach young children about God and our faith. It had been my long-time dream upon retirement to teach as a volunteer, in order to give back to God all His goodness and generosity to our family. I couldn't wait for that time to be with the young children to inculcate in their young minds that there is a God who loves them: to know Him, to love Him, to serve Him and be with Him in heaven.

Thankfully, Stephen had also set his own goals upon retirement. Because of his current service in our parish church as an Acolyte or Minister of the Altar, he planned to visit sick patients in the hospital and read to them the Gospel of Jesus Christ and give them the Holy communion. And I planned to assist him to read the Word of God, and then he explains it to the patient before giving the Holy Communion.

Through the blessings of the Lord, Stephen previously had the opportunity to minister the Holy Communion to the sick at home who were unable to attend the Sunday Mass. And of course, I'd assisted him by reading the Word of God.

At this time of retirement, our mission will be the sick and dying patients in the hospital. In addition to this, while in the room, both of us agreed to check on the flowers given to the patients by visitors; just to clean them up, remove the dead leaves and wilted flowers and arrange them looking fresh again. In this way, we are very sure the patient will be brightened up, physically and spiritually at the same time. Two birds in one stone! So, we are a team doing together this noble mission of serving God in every little way we can!

Mr. Carlton, one of the inspirational speakers about retirement said, "List down all the activities you love and enjoy doing. As a couple, agree on some that you can do together."

Having fun together definitely enhances the couple's positive emotions which magically creates ripple effects towards good relationship, unity and mainly overcome differences and fosters hope when another challenge arise. Very true indeed! If this is the case, then there would be no problems or issues at all with retired couples. In cases of clashing of interest, the easiest resolution is to accept, respect, and support each other.

The couple's differences in personality and interest come in as crucial elements in order to enjoy retirement. Luckily, Stephen and I both love gardening! So, this passion made it easier for us to patch up our differences or even arguments on some occasions. I usually do the easy bits like watering the plants, pulling the weeds and removing the dead leaves, while he carries out the backbreaking process of gardening like clearing and cultivating the soil. I know, I'm so blessed with his endurance in working and beautifying our garden into a state-like landscape of trimmed hedges of murraya jasmine, commonly called as orange jasmine and well-maintained lawn, which showcase his artistic talent and creativity. His eyes gleam with sparkles of joy and the glow on his face reflects the pride of his expertise, every time a passer-by gives uplifting compliments on his beautiful garden!

Stephen is a fanatic fisherman, unfortunately, I'm not. But I love eating fish, my favourite!

So, he usually goes fishing in the afternoon and stays overnight. He adores his most-loved spot where he goes at night because he feels that he owns the place by himself. So, I respect his passion for fishing and I totally surrender him to God for safety and protection; just patiently waits for him to come home in the early morn, with the hope of substantial catch in order to feel once again the pride and joy of his fishing expedition to the fullest. He kept saying that he's surrounded by angels and I didn't need to worry at all. The vast ocean naturally provides him endless fresh air which is therapeutic for his chronic bronchitis, that why he calls it as his "heaven's natural therapy." The smell of the sea breeze and splash of the salty water makes him feel like he's in paradise, coinciding with the thrill of feeling the fish being caught as he pulls it struggling for its freedom and lifts it up in the air and secure it as his own trophy! What a life! Praise God for this bounty!

"Let's put up a business together once we'd reached retirement!" were the words of Frank, who was one of our closest friends in the neighbourhood. Sadly, he passed away three years ago without achieving that goal. During that particular day, when he uttered those words, made me wonder why people still focused on working and earning money even at the stage of retirement? Is this the main reason for living? Stephen and I explained to him gently all our set goals and he just shrugged his shoulders. Since then, we haven't heard from him.

One night, unexpectedly his wife Lita called us with her anxious-hysterical voice and sadly told us about Frank's deteriorating health and desperately wanted to see us. Hastily, we walked downhill towards their two-storey house and paid him a visit. I'd noticed his gladness to see us and slowly had spoken the words of forgiveness as he confessed his resentment towards us regarding our retirement plans. We felt so sorry for him, hugged him and together we prayed the Rosary holding hands like brothers and sisters! After two days, Frank passed away, gone to his eternal home. May his soul rest in peace! Amen.

Truly, retirement is the most rewarding and exciting chapter of our life to serve God to the fullest, with goals set before reaching it! However, serving God is still possible even during younger years. This sets no limit; grab every chance when it comes. As another quotation I'd noticed posted at a retirement village's lobby states, "Retirement is not the end of the road, but the beginning of the open highway." Hence, it is the golden opportunity to serve God completely with love, peace and joy in our hearts, until that most coveted prize of beatific vision takes place gloriously!

3. Pandemic: Blessings and Challenges

June 2020 – March 2022

The big challenge now was this COVID 19 virus, which stopped the normal flow of life. It certainly, interrupted and halted our goals and planned activities for our retirement, which caused emotional, mental, and social chaos in our daily lives.

Stephen and I both agreed to heighten up and intensify our spirituality in order to combat the depressing situations happening globally. Restrictions were issued by the government like, hospital visitations, social distancing upon entering all indoor supermarkets, department stores and even places of worship, while also wearing masks. Schools were closed and students stayed home for online learning. These unexpectedly affected the execution of our projected activities and plans on 'what to do upon retirement!' We were not even allowed to go out, except for essential reasons, like a quick-drop-go to the grocery, chemist and doctor.

With the help of modern technology like Zoom, Skype, Messenger Chat, Google Meet and others, communication and learning are still possible. I joined the two-months training of being a catechist through our parish coordinator, conducted by the Diocese. The training was held through Zoom meetings. After two-months of faithful and diligent attendance, I officially finished the Level 1 Special Religious Education training. Praise God!

On several occasions, our whole family met up on FaceTime in order to see each other and give updates on our own respective activities. On birthdays, we'd FaceTime to greet the celebrant and sing the birthday song as the candle on a cake is blown followed by cheers, laughter and lots of love! We managed to be closer, though far from each other through modern technology. I've noticed too, that even relatives and friends from far places had the chance to see each other after many years of zero communication. Truly, this is the blessing of technology, distance is no longer a hindrance to communicate and set eyes upon each other. This pandemic, after all, gave way to a closer and loving relationship among families, relative, and friends. It absolutely helped long-time friends and relatives to catch up and give updates on their respective family activities, which livened up their weakened and lost touch of communication.

Staying at home meant a lot for couples! It's either a make-up or break-up! With our own experience, Stephen and I managed to be together twenty-four hours a day and seven days a week! I must admit, it wasn't that easy! After 46 years of being married, we also experienced our ups and downs in our relationship, which was considered normal according to marriage counsellors. But one most important aspect in our marriage is the presence of God in the midst of us. When we would encounter a disagreement during the day, we made sure, that we'd made up before the sun goes down and that's always upon the conclusion of our nightly Rosary prayers. As the saying goes, "The family that prays together, stays together." This has proven valid and true in our marital relationship, which lasted us these forty-six years and still going.

Unfortunately, some couples didn't cope being together for the 24/7 period at home. They ended up either separated or divorced. They weren't able to survive the enclosed dwelling of deafening silence and indifference, with just the two of them the whole day and night.

Hopefully, in God's time, these couples will see the light of reconciliation and one day be together again as one.

Stephen and I are both active in serving our parish and look forward for the total ease of restrictions, so we can fully execute our projected plans and be of service to the sick people in the hospital and I can freely teach the young children about God and our faith. We look forward for a full service towards others, for we both believe this is the way God planned us to be as a couple, to serve together like the two intertwined hearts, honouring, praising, thanking, and glorifying the Lord, forever together!

God gave us so much, so we just want to give back any tiny act of love we could, to show our endless gratitude to HIS unconditional love, divine providence, guidance and protection to us and most of all towards our children and their children's future children!

4. The Honour and Splendour of Retirement

Do you know what I love best about being retired? There is no more rushing and chasing our own tails! I wouldn't hear anymore the repetitive words of hubby, "Hurry up, we're running late!" Freedom from the hustle and bustle of everyday activities revolving around office works, household chores, school and children's activities as well as their extra-curricular undertakings like in sports, music, dancing, etc. All through the years, Stephen and I tackled the hurdles of each day's challenges like the growing pains of our children during their teenage years, our own trials at work, and the financial struggles on the record-breaking 18% home loan interest rate in the 1990's, just to mention a few. But God never sleeps and faithfully looks at our hearts. With every pain we'd suffered which struck our hearts, sprouted the seeds of victory and glory, through God's divine providence!

When we retired in May 2020, Stephen and I decided to install two modern-window shutters in our bedroom in preparation for the coming winter. On an early Saturday morning, an old man wearing a fashionable leather jacket with an akubra hat on, like that of Paul Hogan's, knocked at our door holding a very old-fashioned brief case. As I'd seen him through the intercom-camera, I hastily opened the door and he said that he was the sales representative from the window shutter company. He politely introduced himself as Rod and straight away proudly presented himself as an 80 years old man, still strong and kicking!

Of course, we were astonished and shocked at his age, so we eagerly asked him his secrets, as he sat down comfortably and in turn cheerfully gave us lecture about life's retirement.

Rod proudly shared his wisdom about retirement. He said, "To retire doesn't mean to withdraw from active life, socially, physically, mentally and spiritually. The usual activities remain the same with the huge difference of slowing down the pace, particularly our movements. Retirement simply means to re-tyre;

to change our tyres just like the vehicle tyres into a lighter and slower speed! Maybe change our tyre from Bridgestone brand to Dunlop or any other lighter tyre. Our body is like a motor; it shouldn't stop its movements, otherwise, it will be stuck or jammed. That's why, it is important to remain active in a moderate pace, at the same time loving and enjoying the projects or ventures we do. If that's the case, isn't it like we're in paradise or on holidays? This is actually what I feel, hence, I'm still working. Just under my own terms and conditions!" Then he laughed and we vibrantly clapped our hands as warm appreciation of that beautiful advice! He opened his briefcase and pulled out all the brochures ready to work and explain his product.

The joy and honour of retirement means being respected by almost everyone you meet along, whether on the road, shopping centres, markets, or even in church, which is just superbly priceless! It is a hard-earned effort, but such a humbling experience to reach this most significant part of our lives. Being retirees, our hearts almost burst with overwhelming gratitude whenever someone gives up his seat for us or offers assistance when carrying a heavy package or simply guide us to the first spot in a very long queue. Such is the honour and splendour of being a retiree!

This is the paramount time to spend quality time with our children and grandchildren, especially in going to church together in special occasions like birthdays, anniversaries to give our praises and thanksgiving before breaking bread at home or restaurants. This is the glorious time when our children show their utmost love and care every time they drop by to let us taste their home cooked food or invite us over for dinner. The respectable and loving treatment they've shown to us, as their aging parents is beyond our expectations.

They don't allow us to drive anymore, but always count us as passengers whenever a holiday trip is organised. We feel like royalty!

We had graduated from one chapter in our lives and we proudly opened a brand-new one, which I consider the most rewarding one! You may ask, "Why?" "This is the ultimate time when we stop living at work and start working for living," as quoted from a poster I'd seen from one government agency. This is the best time to reflect and thoroughly identify the purpose and meaning of life and mainly to do the many things which make us happy with the beloved spouse. I knew very well the reasons why I'm here on earth since I was in elementary grade, but maturity deepens and extends the visions of life's in-depth meaning and purpose.

Retirement is the most awaited time of finishing the line in our journey for the glory of Christ. Grab every opportunity to serve God in the face of every person we meet who needs help in any way we could possibly extend. This is the time to give back God's goodness and make the most of our lives to be fruitful, meaningful and spirit-filled one. This is the supreme time to treasure every moment like gold to be with God "24/7" by loving Him, and serving Him all for His honour and glory!

Let me quote the words of wisdom from Sister Clair, a German nun, whom I met in 1975 when she said, "There are two most important days in our lives: One is the day when we were born; the other is the day when we found out why!" The right time has come for me to do what I love and enjoy doing; gardening, teaching, writing reflections and journals of my dreams and visions. The ultimate goal is weaving together all the threads in my journals into a book in order to proclaim God's unconditional love and faithfulness to His people. That's why, with the blessings and graces from our Lord God Almighty, this testimonial book came into fruition in the right time and in the best of time which is GOD'S TIME! Amen! Amen! Amen!

"Rejoice always, pray without ceasing and give thanks to God at every moment. This is the will of God for you in Christ Jesus." (1 Thessalonians 5:16-18)

And on that day, you will say, "Give thanks to the Lord, acclaim His name; make known His deeds among the nations, and proclaim how exalted is His name" Sing praises to the Lord, for His works are glorious; let this be known over the earth. (Isaiah 12:4-5)

At this point ends my journey of 46 years after… "The Sign," which revealed that momentous part of my life on how I received "The Sign" from the Holy Spirit and faithfully followed His plan for me. I hope you've enjoyed it and learned some lessons which you may be able to use in your personal journey.

Till we meet again in my next episodes through God's graces and blessings.

May God bless and hold you always in the palm of His hands! Amen!

Lanni Fides

Conclusion

Did you enjoy the ride in my life's journey?

God immensely manifested His great love towards this orphaned girl from childhood to the present time of her journey. God continuously hovered around her through the guidance and enlightenment of the Holy Spirit, especially in the crosswords of her life and when she found herself drowning. God gently and lovingly picked her up and showed her the right way and gave her "The Sign."

I humbly opened to you my life's story, with the main purpose of proclaiming God's unconditional love and faithfulness to His people. This is a concrete example of this truth found in this testimonial book of my journey -- 46 years after... "The Sign," which I can gratefully and proudly call a blissful marriage.

It is my sincerest hope that you've found enjoyment and took some good 'take-aways' from my story, which hopefully would help you in your day-to-day challenges!

Whether single or married, separated or divorced, I firmly entreat you to reflect the importance of this acronym **'SPIRIT.'**

S – spiritual life – deepen your relationship with Jesus as your friend and God as your father and the Holy Spirit as your guide. Constantly have a conversation with God. In every decision in life, always seek the guidance of the Holy Spirit, in order to be directed to the right path.

P – prayer life – pray always and make it a habit like your morning coffee and programmed daily exercise. Prayers everyday keep you away from wrong doings and lead you to a peaceful life.

I – intimacy – express your innermost feeling and have intimate relationship with God, who is always ready to listen and help you unconditionally.

R – reconciliation/repentance – reconcile arguments and differences with spouse or anyone, most especially with God when committed wrong-doings. The humble word 'sorry' is the magic word combined with sincere repentance which cleanses and purifies your heart.

I – interest- for married couples: endeavour to have same interest and activities as a couple and serve together in the community or in the church in any small way you could. For the singles:

join groups with the same faith and be active in the mission of the Church.

T - thanksgiving – express thanksgiving in prayers regularly. Always thank the Lord for everything, in any circumstances.

Finally, I would like to sincerely thank you for spending time in reading this book, which I hope served my aim of proclaiming God's love and faithfulness to His people!

Before I close this, let me share this wonderful quotation from Saint Teresa of Calcutta:

"Profound joy of the heart is like a magnet which indicates the path of life."

Rest assured that you are in my prayers and please include me too in your prayers.

See you again in the next book I will be writing as the Holy Spirit leads me. God bless you!

Lanni Fides
16 May 2022

"So realise that the Lord, your God,

is indeed the True and Faithful God.

He is loyal to His covenant,

and His love reaches to the thousandth generation

of those who love Him and fulfill His commandments."

(Deuteronomy 7:9)

About the Author

Lanni Fides is a former high school teacher-librarian and college professor who migrated from the Philippines to Australia with her family in 1988. In 1991, the family joined Couples for Christ, NSW Australia, became a couple-leader of a mission team to the northern region of Couples for Christ, and a coordinator of NSW Handmaids of the Lord, a ministry for women of the community. Currently, she is still an active member of the seniors' group in her community.

As a retiree, she's an active parishioner of St. John 23rd Parish, Stanhope Gardens, NSW, and a catechist of the state schools of the parish under the Ministry of Special Religious Education of the Diocese.

Her mission in writing books is to proclaim God's unconditional love and faithfulness to His people. Her first book entitled: Encounters with God through Dreams and Visions was recently published last month of April this year 2022.

"The Lord's love abides unceasingly; his compassion is never exhausted. Every morning, it is renewed, so great is his faithfulness." (Lamentations 3:22-23)

Truly, God is faithful forever!

Lanni Fides
16 May 2022

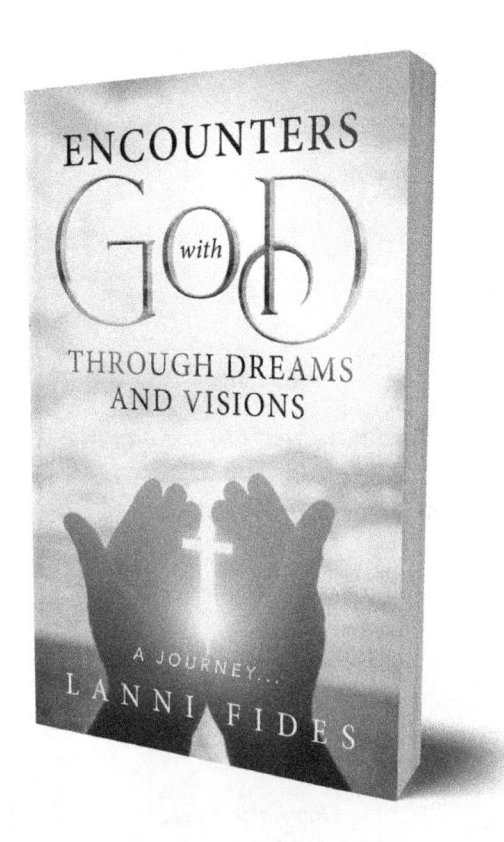

Have you ever wondered why we dream at night and sometimes experience visions? God loves us so much and speaks to us, even at night! This book validates this truth. It is a journey of experiences of some notable characters from the ancient days to the early twentieth century on dreams and visions where God conveys His message and instructions to His people! Are you aware that you may be spiritually gifted? Do you want to find out and discover for yourself this priceless treasure? Then take time to read this book. Hold onto God's power like I did as I revealed my own personal encounters with God through dreams and visions, followed by my interpretations and realisations which directed me and my whole family to the right path of life. Enjoy the journey with God!

---

amazon.com
chapters.indigo.ca
barnesandnoble.com
booktopia.com.au

"Worthy are You, Oh Lord and God,

to receive glory, honour and power!

For You have created all things;

by Your will they were created

and have their existence!"

(Revelation 4:11)

"May God be praised forever"

CPSIA information can be obtained
at www.ICGtesting.com
Printed in the USA
BVHW041335270622
640732BV00001B/5

9 780228 879077